THE KITCHEN LIBRARY

CHICKEN DISHES

INCLUDING

TURKEY, DUCK & GAME

THE KITCHEN LIBRARY

CHICKEN DISHES

INCLUDING
TURKEY, DUCK & GAME

Clare Ferguson

OCTOPUS BOOKS

CONTENTS

This edition published 1988 by
Octopus Books Limited
59 Grosvenor Street, London W1
Reprinted 1988
© Cathay Books 1984
ISBN 0 7064 3242 8

Printed by Mandarin Offset in Malaysia

INTRODUCTION

Recipes for chicken are to be found in almost every culture. In the past poultry was expensive and very seasonal. Roasting chickens were usually male; hens were kept for laying, becoming available later as boiling fowl; turkeys, ducks and geese were for special occasions. Today, many new types and smaller cuts of poultry have become available, fresh and frozen, which are easy and quick to cook.

Though plump and tender, today's birds somewhat lack the farmyard savour of the past and it is a challenge to invent exciting seasonings, sauces, dressings, marinades, stuffings and accompaniments to make poultry more delicious than ever!

Game birds and animals too are more readily available. Super-efficient selection and production practices now mean that they come on sale suitably matured and beautifully prepared, often trussed and barded with fat or bacon.

This exciting cookbook includes ways to spit-roast, barbecue, spatchcock, grill, poach, braise and fricassé, plus original and traditional ways to pan-fry, bake, stew, make rillettes, spreads, pies, soups, stocks and sauces.

Whether you try a hot chicken sandwich, Thanksgiving turkey, rabbit pie or a sophisticated pheasant dish, enjoy preparing it and eating it.

NOTES

Standard spoon measurements are used in all recipes
1 tablespoon = one 15 ml spoon.
1 teaspoon = one 5 ml spoon.

Fresh herbs are used unless otherwise stated. If unobtainable substitute a bouquet garni of the equivalent dried herbs, or use dried herbs instead but halve the quantities stated.

Use freshly ground black pepper where pepper is specified.

All poultry and game specified are fresh or thoroughly thawed frozen birds unless otherwise stated. All weights given are for oven-ready birds unless otherwise stated.

For all recipes, quantities are given in both metric and imperial measures. Follow either set but not a mixture of both, because they are not interchangeable.

Cooking terms are basic recipes marked with an asterisk are explained on pages 6 to 13.

POULTRY CLASSIFICATION

Chickens are available from as small as 600 g (1¼ lb), sold as poussins, up to 3 kg (7 lb) when they are known as capons. In between come broiling and roasting chickens, often sold under the general heading 'roasting'.

Fresh birds usually have the best of flavour, but frozen poultry tastes perfectly acceptable as long as it is thawed completely before cooking. If poultry is not thawed properly, there is a great risk of food poisoning. Thawing times vary depending on the size of bird and the temperature at which it is defrosted. It should be thawed in a cool place. As a guide, allow 1-3 days for turkey and goose, 24 hours for chicken and duck, and 6 to 8 hours for poultry portions.

Poussins: Delicate baby chickens weighing between 350-625 g (12 oz-1¼ lb). They cook quickly and are very tender. One poussin generally serves 1 person.

Broilers: Tender, immature chickens 1-1.5 kg (2-3½ lb) in weight. They are also called 'spring chickens' and may be only 8 weeks old. They are particularly suitable for grilling and frying.

Roasting chickens: Mature birds of 1-3 kg (2-7 lb) in weight. Broilers are often sold as roasting chickens.

Capons: Large-breasted, tender, very meaty chickens, also called super chickens, 2.25 kg-3 kg (5-7 lb) in weight. These birds are now super-fed before adulthood to achieve their size. They are suitable for most cooking methods.

Boiling Fowl: Older, often tougher, but flavourful chickens, up to 3 kg (7 lb) in weight. Best kept for moist methods of cooking, e.g. poaching, stewing, soups and stocks. Also known as casserole hens.

Turkey: These can weigh anything from 2.25-11.5 kg (5-26 lb). Average weight is 4.5-6 kg (10-14 lb).

Ducks: Ducklings generally weight 1.5-1.75 kg (3½-4 lb) and ducks 1.75-2.75 kg (4-6 lb). One serves 2-4 people.

Geese: These bony birds weigh 3-6.5 kg (7-15 lb).

TRUSSING

Trussing keeps the bird in a compact shape which promotes an even rate of cooking. It also makes the handling of the bird easier, e.g. for browning. Most birds, other than large turkeys and geese, can be trussed simply with string:

Using about 1 metre (3 ft) of string, place the bird (stuffed or otherwise) back downwards with the centre of the string beneath its tail end. Cross the string over the tail and loop each end around the opposite drumstick, pulling the ends away from the bird to bring the drumsticks over the vent.

Turn the bird on to its breast. Dealing with one end of the string at a time, take it up the length of the thigh and loop it

around the upper wing then across the neck flap. Repeat the process on the opposite side then knot the strings at the centre of the back. Tighten neck string if necessary.

If bacon or barding fat is required, lay this criss-cross or straight over the breast. Take excess string across the breast to secure the fat firmly, knot and cut off ends.

CLASSIC ROASTING

Roasting can be done at a high or low temperature, covered or uncovered. Barding with bacon or pork fat is usually advisable, though some birds are now self-basting; always follow pack instructions. Stuffing or forcemeat is optional; it helps give moisture and flavour to long-cooked birds, acts as a 'meal extender' and provides texture and flavour contrast. The fat present in suet, butter, bacon or sausage meat used in stuffings helps with internal basting. Do not pack stuffing too tight. Vary your stuffings with part-cooked rice, vegetables, nuts, fruit, lemon or orange rind. Bacon rolls and chipolata accompaniments can be cooked around the bird part way through cooking.

To test if cooked: Pierce the thickest part of the lower thigh: if the juices run clear golden yellow the bird is cooked.

For very large birds, insert a meat thermometer in the thigh. The bird is cooked when the temperature reaches 88-98°C (180-190°F), depending on taste.

TO JOINT A CHICKEN OR DUCK

1. Hold the chicken up by its wings, snap and cut off wings at shoulder joints so that some breast meat is attached to upper wing joints.
2. Place chicken on its back with tail end towards you. Cut skin between carcass and legs, then bend legs back until the joints show. Snap and sever joints. Cut through flesh between these and the pelvic area.

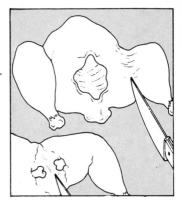

3. Pull skin up tightly over thighs, then cut down to 'knee' joint. Snap and sever the joint, giving 2 thigh and 2 drumstick portions.
4. Turn breast uppermost and, using a knife or poultry shears, cut across carcass and down behind ribcage to the centre of the backbone. Bend the tail section back, then snap and cut it free. Flatten the lower back section if wished.

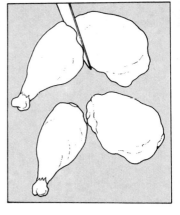

5. Use a knife or poultry shears to separate the front and back sections, cutting from inside; leave most meat on the breast section. Flatten the back section by breaking the rib bones.
6. Slide the neck skin back from the upper breast to locate the wishbone. Make small cuts into the flesh, expose, cut and pull out the bone by its joint, cutting it free at the two ends.

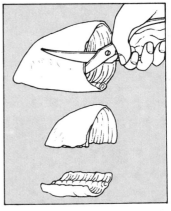

7. Flatten the breast section with the palm of your hand and cut in half down its length, or crossways if preferred.

8

TO BONE A CHICKEN OR TURKEY FOR STUFFING AND ROLLING

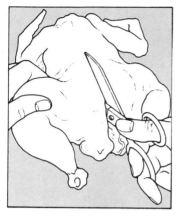

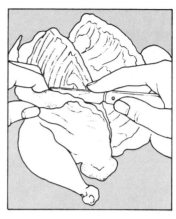

1. Using poultry shears or strong kitchen scissors, cut the bird in half down one side of the backbone.

2. Open out flat, skin side down, and with a small sharp knife, scrape free the flesh from the backbone and ribs, exposing the bones as cleanly as possible.

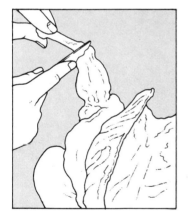

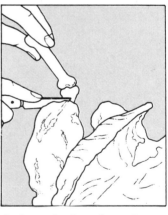

3. Snap the wing joints and turn the wings inside out, freeing the bone completely, cut through the sinews but leave the wing tips complete. Cut forwards to avoid damaging the skin.

4. Snap the legs from their ball and socket joints and cut through the connecting tissues to free them. Turn them inside out and remove the bones.

5. Cut through the tail and tail bone.
Use all the bones to make stock (see page 11).

FLAVOURING FOR POULTRY AND GAME

Bouquet garni Bay leaf, parsley and thyme tied together in a piece of muslin with string. Variety can be achieved by adding any of the following: sage, lemon balm, tarragon, chervil, rosemary, lovage, mint, winter savory, fennel or marjoram.

Other herbs, often best used on their own and delicious with poultry, are basil, chives, sorrel and mint.

Aromatics good with poultry and game are: dried orange and lemon peel; green, pink, white and black peppercorns; cayenne pepper, chilli powder and paprika; fresh root ginger, star anise, five-spice powder, soy sauce and oyster sauce; nutmeg, mace, cinnamon, cardamom, dill, cumin and coriander. Garlic, shallots, onions, spring onions and leeks are, of course, indispensable.

Wines, ciders and flavoured vinegars are invaluable. Try to avoid harsh substitutes: white vinegar, for example, will never achieve the same delightful taste as raspberry vinegar. Lemon juice, however, is a useful substitute for delicate vinegars in most cases.

Ready-prepared seasonings, such as seasoned salts, peppers, mustards, dressings and mayonnaise, can be used in some recipes.

Oils Various oils are used in cooking and marinades. Olive oil gives a mellow flavour but one which is not always preferable, so do follow the recipes.

10

Chicken, Turkey or Duck Stock

2 kg (4½ lb) carcasses, trimmings, gizzards necks and hearts
2.75 litres (5 pints) water
juice of 1 lemon
3 carrots, halved
3 onions, each stuck with 2 cloves
3 celery sticks, halved
1 leek, halved lengthways
bouquet garni
8 peppercorns
1-2 tablespoons salt

Trim away the tough gizzard skin, slice the meat, cut the neck in several places and halve the heart. Place the carcasses, trimmings and giblets in a large pan. Add the water, lemon juice, vegetables, herbs and peppercorns. Bring to the boil, skim, then simmer for 2½ hours, skimming occasionally. Season with salt to taste. Strain and chill for 8 hours; remove the fat. Store in the refrigerator for up to 4 days.

For a stronger flavour, boil briskly, uncovered, until well reduced.

Makes 1.5-1.75 litres (2½-3 pints)

Chicken Soup: Pass the stock through a fine sieve or muslin to clarify. To each 600 ml (1 pint), add 3-4 tablespoons cider or white wine, or the juice of 1 lemon. Bring to the boil and season liberally with salt and pepper.

If a thicker soup is preferred, work 1 tablespoon each butter and flour to a smooth paste and gradually add to the soup, stirring constantly over low heat until thickened. Stir in 150 ml (¼ pint) milk or single cream and heat gently.

Game Stock

25 g (1 oz) butter
50 g (2 oz) bacon
3 onions, sliced
4 leeks, sliced
3 celery sticks, sliced
3 carrots, sliced
250 g (8 oz) pie venison or other game, cubed
1 kg (2 lb) game carcasses
6 black peppercorns
6 juniper berries
bouquet garni
2.25 litres (4 pints) water
salt

Melt the butter in a large heavy-based pan, add the diced bacon and fry until crisp and the fat runs. Add the vegetables and fry until browned. Add the meat and carcasses and fry for 5 to 10 minutes, until browned. Add the peppercorns, juniper berries, bouquet garni, water, and salt to taste. Bring to the boil, skimming 2 or 3 times, lower the heat and simmer for 2 to 2½ hours.

Strain the stock; keep the meat cubes to add to soup if liked (see below). Chill the stock, then remove the fat. Keep in the refrigerator for up to 4 days, using as required.

Makes 1.2-1.5 litres (2-2½ pints)

Game Soup: Proceed as for Chicken soup (above), but flavour the stock with 150 ml (¼ pint) red wine, Madeira or sherry. Add the reserved meat from the stock if wished.

ACCOMPANIMENTS FOR POULTRY AND GAME

Gravy

Pour off all but 2 tablespoons fat from the pan, leaving the residues. Measure 2 tablespoons plain flour into the pan and stir over low heat until bubbling and golden. Gradually stir in 300 ml (½ pint) stock, wine or cider.

Add salt and pepper to taste and, if wished, one of the following for extra flavour: 2 to 4 tablespoons single cream; a few shakes of Worcestershire sauce; 1 tablespoon Dijon mustard; 1 tablespoon redcurrant, quince or rowan jelly.

Finally add 1 to 2 tablespoons brandy, port or dry sherry to transform the gravy into something really special.

Bread Sauce

600 ml (1 pint) milk
1 small onion, grated
pinch each of ground
    cloves and ground
    bay leaves
75 g (3 oz) fresh
    white breadcrumbs
25 g (1 oz) butter
salt
ground nutmeg
	Place the orange and lemon rind and juice, and the redcurrant jelly in a almost to boiling point. Stir in the breadcrumbs and butter. Remove from the heat and leave for 5 minutes. Add salt and nutmeg to taste.
	    Serve with roast chicken and turkey.
	Serves 4 to 6

Cumberland Sauce

finely grated rind and
    juice of 1 orange
    and 1 lemon
250 g (8 oz)
    redcurrant jelly
4 tablespoons port
1 teaspoon arrowroot
    blended with
    1 tablespoon water
    (optional)
	Place the orange and lemon rind and juice, and the redcurrent jelly in a pan, bring to the boil and boil until the jelly has dissolved. Add the port and simmer for 5 minutes. If wished, thicken with the blended arrowroot.
	    Serve with chicken or turkey.
	Serves 4 to 6

Gooseberry Sauce

250 g (8 oz)
    gooseberries,
    chopped
4 tablespoons cider or
    white wine
25 g (1 oz) butter
25 g (1 oz) caster
    sugar
	Place the gooseberries and cider or wine in a pan and simmer for about 10 minutes, until soft. Add the butter and sugar and stir until dissolved. Work in a food processor or electric blender or sieve, until smooth.
	    Serve with roast goose or duck.
	Serves 4 to 6

Fried Breadcrumbs

50 g (2 oz) bacon fat	Heat the fat and butter in a small pan,
25 g (1 oz) butter	add the breadcrumbs and toss over
75 g (3 oz) fresh	high heat until crisp. Season with the
white breadcrumbs	salt and cayenne and drain on kitchen
1/4 teaspoon salt	paper. Serve hot.
pinch of cayenne	**Serves 3 to 4**

Game Chips

500 g (1 lb) old	Soak the potatoes in salted water for
potatoes, thinly	1 hour. Drain, dry very thoroughly
sliced	and deep-fry small quantities at a time
oil for deep-frying	in hot oil for 2 to 3 minutes until light
sea salt or seasoned	golden. Drain on kitchen paper. Just
salt	before serving fry again for 2 to
	3 minutes until very crisp. Drain
	and sprinkle with salt to serve.
	Serves 4 to 6

Matchstick Potatoes: Proceed as for game chips but cut potatoes into match-like strips.

Potato Purée

500 g (1 lb) potatoes,	Using a food processor, mouli or
boiled	sieve, work the potatoes to a smooth
50 g (2 oz) butter	purée. Beat in the butter, cream, and
2 tablespoons thick	salt and pepper to taste. Serve very
cream	hot.
salt and white pepper	**Serves 3 to 4**

Other Vegetable Purées: Sweet potatoes, turnips, peas, parsnips, carrots, celeriac and chestnuts can be treated similarly or mixed half and half with potato. To vary, use bacon fat instead of butter, nutmeg instead of pepper.

To serve, mould using oiled ramekins or timbales; or mound, pressing down on a serving spoon to form ovals.

Sauté Potatoes

500 g (1 lb) par-	Cut the potatoes into 5 mm (1/4 inch)
boiled potatoes	thick slices. Heat the butter and oil in
40 g (1 1/2 oz) butter	a large heavy-based frying pan, add
2 tablespoons olive	the potatoes and fry until golden and
oil	crisp on both sides, turning carefully.
salt and pepper	Sprinkle with salt, pepper and herbs
chopped chives and/	to taste to serve.
or parsley	**Serves 3 to 4**

Surprise Spring Chicken

2 limes
1 small onion, cut
  into 8 slices
1 × 1-1.25 kg
  (2-2½ lb) spring
  chicken
25 g (1 oz) raisins
2 tablespoons olive
  oil
pinch of chilli powder
sea salt
lime and onion slices
  to garnish

Slash one lime almost through in 8 places and insert an onion slice in each cut. Place inside the chicken cavity with the raisins.

Squeeze the juice from the remaining lime and mix with the oil, chilli powder and salt to taste. Pour over the chicken and leave to marinate for 1 hour.

Truss securely* and place in a roasting pan. Cook in a preheated moderately hot oven, 190°C (375°F), Gas Mark 5, for 1½ hours, basting twice, until the juices run clear yellow*.

Serve the chicken, with its juices, on a bed of noodles tossed in a herb-flavoured butter. Garnish with lime and onion slices.

Serves 2 to 4

Claypot Chicken

1 × 1.5 kg
    (3-3½ lb) roasting
    chicken
salt and pepper
bunch of mixed
    thyme, parsley and
    bay leaves
2 guavas, peeled,
    quartered and
    seeded
2 oranges, peeled and
    thinly sliced
    crossways
2 shallots or 1 small
    onion, chopped
1 tablespoon olive oil
herbs to garnish

Presoak a chicken brick following manufacturer's instructions.

Season the chicken inside and out with salt and pepper and put the herbs inside the body cavity. Truss securely*.

Arrange the guava and orange slices on the base and sides of the chicken brick and place the chicken in the centre. Sprinkle the shallot or onion and olive oil over the chicken and fruit. Cover and cook in a preheated hot oven, 230°C (450°F), Gas Mark 8, for 1¼ to 1½ hours, until the juices run clear yellow*.

Arrange the chicken and fruit slices on a warmed serving dish. Pour over the juices and garnish with herbs. Serve with buttered broccoli.

Serves 4
NOTE: If fresh guavas are unavailable, canned guavas may be used instead.

Ornitha Zante

1 × 1.5 kg
(3-3½ lb) roasting
chicken with
giblets
2 cloves garlic,
crushed
3 tablespoons olive
oil
1 × 397 g (14 oz)
can tomatoes
1 teaspoon dried
oregano
450 ml (¾ pint)
chicken stock* or
water
250 g (8 oz) small
pasta shells or fine
noodles
salt and pepper

Remove the giblets and set aside.
Truss the chicken securely*. Rub the
bird all over with the garlic and some
of the oil. Place in a roasting pan and
surround with the giblets, tomatoes
with their juice, oregano and
1 tablespoon of the oil. Cover loosely
with foil and cook in a preheated
moderate oven, 180°C (350°F), Gas
Mark 4, for 1 to 1¼ hours.

Remove the foil and add the stock
or water and pasta, stirring well so
the pasta is thoroughly moistened.
Dribble the remaining oil over all and
add salt and pepper to taste. Return to
the oven, uncovered, and cook for
45 minutes, until the pasta is plump
and the chicken is very tender.

Serve with okra.

Serves 4

3–Spiced Rotisserie Chicken

2 cloves garlic,
halved
10 black peppercorns,
roughly crushed
salt
1 × 1.75 kg (4 lb)
roasting chicken
1 teaspoon cumin
1 teaspoon turmeric
1 teaspoon paprika
2 tablespoons oil
1 tablespoon white
wine or vinegar

Put the garlic, peppercorns, and salt
to taste inside the cavity of the
chicken. Place it on the rotisserie
skewer and secure with the two-
pronged 'forks' at either end. Switch
on the rotisserie and check that the
bird is centred well, then switch off.

Mix the 3 spices, ½ teaspoon salt
and the oil to a thick paste and spread
half all over the bird. Leave for
2 hours.

Switch on the rotisserie and cook
for 50 minutes on high heat and
15 minutes on low heat. Stir the wine
or vinegar into the remaining paste
and use to baste the chicken
occasionally. Remove from the
skewer and transfer to a warmed
serving dish. Leave to stand for
2 to 3 minutes before carving.

Serve with shredded raw
courgette, mint and yogurt salad.

Serves 4 to 6

Jellied Devon Chicken

1 × 1.25 kg (2½ lb)
    spring chicken
    with giblets
1 prepared pig's
    trotter, halved
    lengthways
2 tablespoons cider
    vinegar
6 marjoram sprigs,
    crushed
1 teaspoon sea salt
20 black peppercorns
15 g (½ oz) gelatine,
    softened in
    2 tablespoons
    cold water
TO GARNISH:
marjoram sprigs
    (optional)
4 lemon twists
4 tablespoons Devon
    clotted cream

Remove giblets and truss chicken*.
Chop the giblets and place in a large
saucepan with the chicken, pig's
trotter, vinegar, marjoram, salt and
peppercorns. Barely cover with water,
bring to simmering point and cook
gently for 2 hours, until very tender.

Carefully lift out the chicken, drain
and place in a 1.75 litre (3 pint) oval
terrine or casserole, breast upwards.
Strain the cooking liquid through a
fine sieve.

Add half the strained cooking
liquid to the gelatine and heat *gently*
until dissolved. Stir in the remaining
cooking liquid. Pour into the terrine,
around the chicken, and garnish with
marjoram if wished. Chill for 4 hours
or until firm.

Garnish with lemon twists and
serve straight from the dish: serve
jelly and chicken together and spoon
over a little cream.
Serves 3 to 4

18

Chicken with Chick Peas

250 g (8 oz) chick
    peas
15 g (½ oz) butter
2 tablespoons olive
    oil
1.5 kg (3½ lb)
    roasting chicken
pinch of powdered
    saffron
¼ teaspoon cayenne
    pepper
2 teaspoons Harissa
    or tomato purée
2 onions, quartered
finely grated rind and
    juice of 1 orange
1 tablespoon orange
    flower water
300 ml (½ pint)
    chicken stock*
salt and pepper
parsley to garnish

Soak the chick peas in cold water to cover for 8 hours; drain well.

Heat the butter and oil in a heavy-based pan, add the chicken and cook, turning occasionally, for about 10 minutes, until brown all over. Add the remaining ingredients, with salt and pepper to taste, cover and simmer for 1½ to 2 hours, until the juices run clear yellow*; add more stock or water if necessary to keep the chick peas covered.

Transfer to a warmed serving dish and sprinkle with parsley to serve.
Serves 4 to 6

Braised Chicken with Calvados

$1 \times 1.25 \, kg \, (2^{1}/_{2} \, lb)$
spring chicken
salt and pepper
25 g (1 oz) butter
*2 tablespoons olive
oil*
*4 rashers back bacon,
derinded and
chopped*
2 carrots, quartered
*1 large onion,
quartered*
*4 tablespoons
Calvados*
*2 Russet or Cox's
apples, peeled,
cored and quartered*
3-4 thyme sprigs
*300 ml (¹/₂ pint) dry
cider*
*142 ml (5 fl oz)
double cream*

Sprinkle the chicken liberally, inside
and out, with salt and pepper. Heat
the butter and oil in a large
flameproof casserole, add the chicken
and cook for 15 minutes, until golden
brown all over, finishing with the
breast upwards. Add the bacon,
carrots and onion for the last
5 minutes.

Warm the Calvados in a ladle, pour
over the chicken and set alight. When
the flames have subsided, add the
apples, thyme and cider. Cover and
simmer gently for 1 hour, spooning
the liquid over the breast
occasionally. Transfer the chicken to
a warmed serving dish; keep warm.

Boil cooking liquid briskly until
reduced by half. Add the cream and
heat gently, stirring until smooth.
Pour the sauce over the chicken.

Serve with a crisp green salad and
crusty French bread.
Serves 3 to 4

Boned Chicken Apicius

2 sets of lambs' brains
(optional)
1 bouquet garni
(optional)
2 tablespoons lemon
juice
salt
600 ml (1 pint)
boiling water
250 g (8 oz) burghul
(cracked wheat)
1-2 tablespoons
chopped basil
leaves
3-4 tablespoons
chopped mint
leaves
8 spring onions,
sliced
3 eggs, soft-boiled for
3 minutes, then
chopped
1 × 50 g (1¾ oz)
can anchovy fillets,
drained and halved
crossways
2 pork fillets
1 × 1.5 kg (3½ lb)
roasting chicken,
boned*
oil for basting

Place the lambs' brains, if using, in a pan, cover with cold water, and add the bouquet garni, if using, one third of the lemon juice, and salt to taste. Cover and simmer for 18 to 20 minutes or until firm. Drain, cool and dice roughly.

Pour the remaining lemon juice and the boiling water over the burghul in a shallow dish. Add salt to taste, stir and leave for 30 minutes. Drain, then stir in the basil, mint, spring onions, eggs, brains, if using, and anchovy fillets.

Using a food processor, electric blender or mincer, finely mince 1 pork fillet and stir into half the burghul mixture.

Place the boned chicken skin side down on a sheet of heavy-duty foil. Smooth the pork mixture over the surface, fitting it evenly into the leg and wing cavities. Cover with the remaining burghul mixture and place the remaining whole pork fillet lengthways down the centre. Roll up the chicken and secure the overlapped edges with wooden cocktail sticks or skewers and string, or use a trussing needle and string. Turn the chicken over so that the join is underneath and secure the legs and wings close to the body with skewers. Rub all over with oil.

Place in a roasting pan and cook in a preheated moderate oven, 180°C (350°F), Gas Mark 4, for 2 hours. Leave to stand for 2 to 3 minutes in a warm place, then carve into thick slices. Pour the pan juices over each serving.

This delicious dish is excellent served with vegetable purées* and carrot julienne.
Serves 6 to 8

Illustrated on inside front cover

Feast Day Chicken

1 × 1.5-1.75 kg
    (3-4 lb) roasting
    chicken
salt and pepper
2 shallots, sliced
16 pitted prunes
50 g (2 oz) blanched
    almonds
small thyme sprig
300 ml (½ pint) dry
    cider
    (approximately)
1 tablespoon
    cornflour
4 tablespoons water
1 tablespoon lemon
    juice
TO GARNISH:
12 almonds
parsley sprigs

Sprinkle the chicken inside and out with salt and pepper. Put the shallots, 10 prunes, the almonds and thyme inside the chicken. Truss securely*, place in a deep flameproof casserole and pour in enough cider to cover the legs and part-cover the breast. Cover and cook in a preheated moderate oven, 160°C (325°F), Gas Mark 3, for about 1½ hours or until very tender. Place the chicken on a warmed serving dish.

Boil the cooking liquid rapidly on top of the stove until reduced by a third. Blend the cornflour with the water and lemon juice, add to the casserole and stir until thickened. Leave until cool.

Halve the remaining prunes, push an almond through each half and 'spike' them to the chicken. Pour the cooled sauce over the chicken as a glaze. Garnish with parsley.
Serves 4 to 6

Hot Chicken Open Sandwiches

6 thick slices rye or
  firm wholewheat
  bread
butter for spreading
1 × 1.5 kg (3-3½ lb)
  chicken, freshly
  roasted
3 rashers streaky
  bacon, cooked and
  chopped
1 ripe avocado,
  peeled, stoned and
  thinly sliced
6 tablespoons French
  dressing
chopped chives,
  parsley or chervil
salt and pepper
SAUCE (optional):
3 tablespoons mango
  chutney
3 tablespoons lemon
  mayonnaise

Warm the bread slightly and spread
with the butter.

While the chicken is still hot, pull
off and chop up the crisp skin and lay
it over the bread. Pull the flesh from
the bird in large strips and lay over
the skin. Arrange the bacon and
avocado slices on top. Spoon
1 tablespoon French dressing over
each 'sandwich' and sprinkle with
herbs, and salt and pepper to taste.

To make the sauce, if using, fold
the chutney into the mayonnaise.

Serve the open sandwiches hot,
with crisp lettuce and the sauce, if
wished, as a lunch or supper dish.
Serves 6
NOTE: Sesame hamburger buns, pitta
bread or French bread could also be
used for the base.

Poulet Père Dudu

25 g (1 oz) butter
1 tablespoon olive oil
1 × 1.5 kg (3 lb)
   roasting chicken
1 whole head of
   garlic, trimmed
150 ml (¼ pint)
   Muscadet or other
   dry white wine
250 g (8 oz) shallots,
   sliced
1 bay leaf
bay leaves to garnish
   (optional)

Heat the butter and oil in a flameproof casserole, add the chicken and sauté all over for 10 minutes. Add the head of garlic (unpeeled), wine, shallots and bay leaf. Bring to simmering point, cover and cook in a preheated moderate oven, 180°C (350°F), Gas Mark 4, for about 1½ hours, until the juices run clear yellow*. Transfer to a warmed serving dish.

Serve several garlic cloves with each portion of chicken; they will be tender and surprisingly mild. Each clove can be slipped from its skin and eaten with a bite of chicken.
Serves 4

Chicken Alexa

1 × 1.5 kg
   (3-3½ lb) roasting
   chicken with
   giblets
65 g (2½ oz) butter
salt and pepper
lovage sprig
   (optional)
2 tablespoons white
   wine
1 onion, sliced
1 tablespoon garam
   masala
1 tablespoon plain
   flour
300 ml (½ pint)
   chicken stock
6 tablespoons double
   cream
2 tablespoons lemon
   juice
1 tablespoon clear
   honey
chopped lovage to
   garnish (optional)

Use the chicken giblets and trimmings to make stock* if wished; keep on one side. Truss the chicken securely*

Spread 25 g (1 oz) of the butter all over the chicken, inside and out, and sprinkle with salt and pepper. Put the lovage, if using, in the cavity. Place on its side in a flameproof dish and add the wine. Roast in a preheated moderate oven, 160°C (325°F), Gas Mark 3, for 1¼ to 1½ hours; turn the chicken halfway through cooking.

Joint* the chicken, place on a warmed serving dish and keep hot.

Melt the remaining butter in the dish on the hob, add the onion and sauté until softened, stirring to scrape up the sediment. Add the garam masala and flour and stir over a low heat for 1 to 2 minutes. Gradually add the stock, stirring. Cook gently for 10 minutes, then stir in the cream, lemon juice and honey; heat through.

Pour over the chicken and garnish with lovage, if using. Serve with rice and tomato and cucumber salad.
Serves 4

Mississippi Braised Chicken

1 × 1.5 kg (3½ lb)
  roasting chicken
  with giblets
25 g (1 oz) butter
1 tablespoon corn oil
1 large onion,
  chopped
2 cloves garlic,
  crushed
2 red peppers, grilled,
  seeded, skinned
  and sliced
300 ml (½ pint)
  chicken stock
salt and pepper·
parsley to garnish

Use the chicken trimmings and
giblets to make stock*; keep on one
side. Truss the chicken securely*.

Melt the butter and oil in a deep,
heavy-based pan, add the chicken and
cook for 15 to 20 minutes, until
golden all over; set aside.

Add the onion and garlic to the pan
and cook until golden, then replace
the chicken, breast downwards. Tuck
the red pepper around the chicken,
pour over the stock and season with
salt and pepper to taste. Cover and
cook gently for 1¼ to 1½ hours; turn
the chicken halfway through
cooking. Joint the chicken*, arrange,
on a warmed dish and keep hot.

Work the onion, red pepper and a
little cooking liquid in a food
processor or blender to a smooth
thick sauce. Pour over the chicken
and garnish with parsley.
Serves 4

Chinese Chicken with Black Beans

2 tablespoons salted
   black beans
1 × 1.5 kg
   (3-3½ lb) roasting
   chicken
1 tablespoon soya
   bean oil
1 teaspoon dark
   sesame oil
6 spring onions,
   sliced diagonally
1-2 red chillies,
   seeded and thinly
   sliced
3 tablespoons dry
   sherry
1 teaspoon sugar
1 tablespoon
   cornflour, blended
   with 3 tablespoons
   water
MARINADE:
25 g (1 oz) root
   ginger, coarsely
   grated
1-2 tablespoons soy
   sauce
pepper
TO GARNISH:
spring onion fans (see
   below)
cucumber slices

Soak the salted black beans in cold water to cover for 20 minutes; drain well and set aside.

Mix the marinade ingredients together, with pepper to taste, and use to coat the chicken inside and out. Put in a roasting bag, tie loosely and place in a roasting pan. Leave for 4 to 6 hours, then make several holes in the bag, following manufacturer's instructions.

Cook in a preheated moderate oven, 180°C (350°F), Gas Mark 4, for 1¼ hours. Remove the chicken from the bag, reserving its contents, and place in the roasting pan. Increase the oven temperature to 200°C (400°F), Gas Mark 6, and cook for a further 25 to 30 minutes, until the juices run clear yellow*.

Meanwhile, heat the oils in a pan, add the spring onions and stir-fry over high heat for 30 seconds. Add the chillies and black beans and cook for 2 minutes. Skim off as much fat as possible from the contents of the roasting bag. Add the remaining liquid to the pan with the sherry and sugar. Stir in the blended cornflour and cook until clear and syrupy.

Carve the chicken and arrange on a warmed serving dish. Pour over the sauce. Garnish with spring onion fans and cucumber slices. Serve with beansprouts, a cucumber salad and plain boiled rice.
Serves 4

Spring onion fans: Trim the tops off the spring onions and remove the root base. Carefully slit both ends, leaving the middle part intact. Leave in a bowl of iced water until the spring onions have opened up into fans.

Baker's Chicken

1 × 2.25 kg (5 lb)
  roasting chicken
  with giblets
50 g (2 oz) butter
4 rosemary sprigs
750 g (1½ lb)
  potatoes, thickly
  sliced
500 g (1 lb) onions,
  thickly sliced
salt and white pepper
450-600 ml
  (¾-1 pint) chicken
  stock*

Remove the giblets from the chicken and chop. Spread a little butter inside the chicken cavity, then add 2 rosemary sprigs. Truss securely*.

Spread half the remaining butter over the base of a roasting pan or casserole. Place the chicken in the centre, with the giblets at one end, and surround with the potato and onion slices. Add the remaining rosemary and season with salt and pepper to taste.

Pour over 450 ml (¾ pint) of the stock and dot the chicken with the remaining butter. Cook in a preheated moderate oven, 180°C (350°F), Gas Mark 4, for 1¾ to 2 hours until tender; add extra stock if necessary to keep the potatoes and onions moist.

Transfer the chicken and vegetables to a warmed serving dish. Serve with green beans and carrots tossed in parsley.
Serves 6 to 8

Chicken Monbazillac

25 g (1 oz) butter
1 tablespoon oil
1 × 1.5 kg
    (3-3½ lb) roasting
    chicken
1 tablespoon plain
    flour
150 ml (¼ pint)
    Monbazillac or
    other medium
    sweet white wine
salt and pepper
125 g (4 oz) button
    mushrooms,
    quartered
125 g (4 oz) button
    onions
2 egg yolks
6 tablespoons double
    cream
bunch of mixed herbs
    to garnish

Heat the butter and oil in a heavy-based pan, until foaming. Place the chicken, breast side down, in the pan and cook for 5 minutes, until golden. Turn and brown the other side. Remove from the pan and set aside.

Add the flour to the pan, stirring to scrape up the sediment, and cook for 1 to 2 minutes. Add the wine, and salt and pepper to taste. Add the mushrooms and onions and return the chicken to the pan. Cover and cook over low heat for 1¼ to 1½ hours. Transfer the chicken to a warmed serving dish and keep hot.

Place the egg yolks and cream in a small basin and stir in a little of the hot cooking liquid. Return to the pan, off the heat, add salt and pepper to taste and tilt the pan to blend. Spoon over the chicken.

Garnish with herbs and serve with petit pois and steamed potatoes tossed in a chive-flavoured butter.
Serves 4

Chicken Minceur with Melon

1 × 1.5 kg (3 lb)
   roasting chicken
   with giblets
finely grated rind and
   juice of 2 limes
2 tarragon sprigs or
   2 teaspoons
   tarragon in
   vinegar, drained
450 ml (¾ pint) hot
   chicken stock
salt and pepper
TO SERVE:
1 charentais melon,
   sliced
¼ head of curly
   endive
lime slices

Use the chicken trimmings and
giblets to make stock* if wished; keep
on one side. Truss the chicken*.

Place the lime rind and juice, the
tarragon and the simmering stock in a
flameproof casserole. Add the
chicken, breast side down, cover and
simmer for 1¾ to 2 hours, until the
juices run clear yellow*; turning the
chicken halfway through cooking.
Cut the chicken into quarters and
leave to cool.

Boil the cooking liquid rapidly on
top of the stove until reduced by half;
leave to cool.

Arrange the melon and endive on a
serving dish and lay the chicken on
top. Spoon over some of the sauce
and hand the rest separately. Garnish
with lime slices.
Serves 4

Somerset Chicken

1 × 1.5 kg
  (3-3½ lb) roasting
  chicken
salt and pepper
15 g (½ oz) butter,
  softened
150 ml (¼ pint)
  cider

NECK STUFFING:
2 rashers smoked
  streaky bacon, de-
  rinded and chopped
1 small potato, boiled
  and mashed
25 g (1 oz) walnuts,
  chopped

CAVITY STUFFING:
125 g (4 oz) pork
  sausage meat
4 tablespoons
  chopped parsley
1 small onion, finely
  chopped
125 g (4 oz) pitted
  prunes

To prepare the neck stuffing, fry the bacon in its own fat until crisp. Mix together the potato, bacon, bacon fat, nuts, and pepper to taste. Set aside.

To prepare the cavity stuffing, form the sausage meat into walnut-sized balls and roll each in parsley. Push a little onion into each prune.

Sprinkle the chicken cavity with salt and pepper and fill with the sausage meat balls and prunes. Fill the neck cavity with its stuffing. Truss securely*, spread all over with the butter and place in a roasting pan.

Cook in a preheated moderately hot oven, 190°C (375°F), Gas Mark 5, for 1¼ hours. Remove chicken and keep warm. Add the cider to the pan and boil rapidly, scraping up all the sediment, until reduced by half.

Carve the chicken and arrange on a warmed serving dish with the stuffing. Hand the sauce separately. Serve with Brussels sprouts.
Serves 4 to 6

Boned Chicken Roulé

1 × 1.5 kg
  (3-3½ lb) roasting
  chicken with
  giblets, boned*
450 ml (¾ pint)
  water
1 onion, chopped
1 bouquet garni
salt and pepper
175 g (6 oz) long-
  grain rice
4 tablespoons oil
125 g (4 oz) chicken
  livers, trimmed
  and halved
250 g (8 oz) button
  mushrooms, sliced
250 g (8 oz) cooked
  ham, cut into strips
2 tablespoons peach
  or mango chutney
1 small cos lettuce
TO GARNISH:
radicchio or lettuce
  leaves
chicory slices
  (optional)
parsley sprigs

Place all the chicken bones and the giblets in a pan with the water, onion, bouquet garni and ½ teaspoon salt. Bring to the boil, cover and simmer for 40 minutes. Strain and reserve the stock, seasoning to taste with salt and pepper.

Cook the rice in the reserved stock for 12 to 15 minutes over a low heat until all the liquid has been absorbed. Transfer to a basin and leave to cool.

Heat half the oil in a pan, add the chicken livers and mushrooms and sauté gently for 2 to 3 minutes. Add to the rice with the ham and chutney; mix well.

Trim the root base of the lettuce so that it can stand, but do not cut the base of the leaves. Pack the rice mixture evenly between the leaves and place in the centre of the boned chicken. Season liberally with salt and pepper. Overlap the skin over the lettuce and secure with wooden cocktail sticks. Turn the bird over and use skewers and string to secure wings and legs close to the body.

Brush all over with the remaining oil and place the chicken, join side down, in a roasting pan. Cook in a preheated moderate oven, 180°C (350°F), Gas Mark 4, for 1¾ hours, basting frequently.

Transfer the chicken to a warmed serving dish, lined with radicchio or lettuce leaves and chicory slices if wished. Leave to stand for 2 to 3 minutes in a warm place. Pour the pan juices into a sauceboat. Carve the chicken into slices and hand the sauce separately.

This boned chicken is delicious served with a tomato and green pepper salad and poppy seed bread.
Serves 6

Poussins Medici

2 poussins, halved
   lengthways
50 g (2 oz) butter
1 tablespoon oil
4 rosemary sprigs
150 ml (¼ pint) red
   wine or port
142 ml (5 fl oz)
   single cream
salt and pepper
rosemary sprigs to
   garnish (optional)

Flatten each poussin half slightly. Heat the butter and oil in a large pan, add the rosemary and poussins, skin side down, and sauté for 8 to 10 minutes or until golden. Turn and cook the other side for 8 to 10 minutes. Transfer the poussins to a warmed serving dish keep warm.

Add the wine to the pan, stirring well to scrape up the sediment. Simmer, uncovered, until reduced by half. Add the cream, and salt and pepper to taste, tilting the pan to mix, and continue cooking gently until a smooth sauce forms. Remove the rosemary.

Pour the sauce over the poussins and garnish with rosemary sprigs if liked. Serve with mange-tout, or a crisp green salad, and sauté potatoes or crusty French bread.

Serves 2 or 4

Honey Glazed Poussins

1 tablespoon thick
   honey
2 cloves garlic,
   crushed
3-4 tablespoons wine
   vinegar
1 tablespoon chopped
   marjoram
4 poussins

Mix the honey, garlic and vinegar
together in a large dish. Put a little
marjoram inside each poussin, place
in the dish and marinate for 2 hours,
turning occasionally.

Drain, place in a roasting pan and
roast in a preheated moderately hot
oven, 200°C (400°F), Gas Mark 6, for
30 minutes. Cover with foil and
continue to cook for 15 minutes.

Serve with an endive and fresh
peach salad, if wished.
Serves 4

Poussins Grande Duchesse

10 dried mushrooms
   (preferably morels),
   soaked in warm
   water for 2 hours
40 g (1½ oz) butter,
   softened
4 chicken livers,
   trimmed and
   quartered
½ teaspoon thyme
½ teaspoon parsley
4 poussins
2 tablespoons brandy
4 tablespoons single
   cream
salt and pepper
TO SERVE:
250 g (8 oz) cooked
   spinach

Drain the mushrooms, strain to
remove any grit, and reserve 4 tablespoons water. Halve 8 mushrooms
and finely chop the remaining two.

Melt 25 g (1 oz) of the butter in a
frying pan, add the mushroom halves
and sauté for 8 to 10 minutes. Add
the chicken livers and cook, stirring
carefully, for 3 to 4 minutes, until
golden on the outside but still
pink inside. Add the herbs and
1 tablespoon of the reserved water.
Spoon a quarter of this mixture into
each poussin, and spread the
remaining butter over them.

Place in a roasting pan and cook in
a preheated moderately hot oven,
190°C (375°F), Gas Mark 5, for
50 minutes. Place the poussins on
one side of the pan and pour in the
brandy, remaining reserved water
and the chopped mushrooms. Stir
well to scrape up the sediment, then
add the cream and heat gently. Season
with salt and pepper to taste.

Transfer the poussins to a warmed
serving dish, lined with the spinach,
and pour over the sauce. Serve with a
parsnip or potato purée*.
Serves 4

Poussins Diabolo

*125 g (4 oz) butter,
    softened*
*½ teaspoon dry
    mustard*
*pinch of cayenne
    pepper*
*1 teaspoon anchovy
    essence or sauce*
*1 teaspoon Worcester-
    shire sauce*
*½ teaspoon celery
    salt*
4 poussins
4 teaspoons capers
*watercress sprigs to
    garnish*

Place the butter in a small bowl, add all the seasonings and beat until well blended. Spread all over the poussins and inside the cavities. Put a teaspoon of capers inside each poussin.

Place in a roasting pan and cook in a preheated moderately hot oven, 190°C (375°F), Gas Mark 5, for 40 to 45 minutes, basting occasionally, until golden brown.

Transfer to a warmed serving dish and garnish with watercress. Serve with toast spread with a parsley-flavoured butter, steamed potatoes, and a watercress and radish salad.
Serves 4

Lemon Poussins Persillades

75 g (3 oz) butter,
softened
finely grated rind and
juice of 2 lemons
4 poussins
4 tablespoons
chopped parsley
2 shallots, chopped
salt and pepper
4 tablespoons dry
white wine
TO GARNISH:
parsley sprigs
lemon twists

Place the butter, lemon rind and juice in a small bowl and beat until well blended. Spread all over the poussins and inside the cavities. Mix the parsley and shallots together and place a spoonful inside each poussin. Sprinkle with salt and pepper to taste, place in a roasting pan and pour a tablespoon of wine over each poussin.

Roast in a preheated moderate oven, 180°C (350°F), Gas Mark 4, for 30 minutes, basting occasionally. Increase the heat to 200°C (400°F), Gas Mark 6, and cook for a further 10 minutes or until well browned and crisp.

Transfer to a warmed serving dish and garnish with parsley and lemon twists. Serve with sauté potatoes and green beans tossed with toasted almonds.
Serves 4

Dijon Chicken en Croûte

4 frozen chicken
   breasts en croûte
milk to glaze
15 g (½ oz) butter
1 small onion, finely
   chopped
2 tablespoons Dijon
   mustard
142 ml (5 fl oz)
   single cream
parsley to garnish

Brush the croûtes with milk to glaze and cook from frozen in a preheated moderately hot oven, 190°C (375°F), Gas Mark 5, following pack instructions.

Melt the butter in a small pan, add the onion and sauté until golden. Stir in the mustard, then add the cream. Simmer for 2 to 3 minutes.

Arrange the chicken croûtes on a warmed serving dish and top with a little sauce; hand the rest separately.

Garnish with parsley and serve with French beans and new potatoes.
Serves 4

Chicken Suprêmes Sancerre

4 × 125 g (4 oz)
   chicken breast
   fillets
salt and pepper
25 g (1 oz) butter
2 rashers streaky
   bacon, derinded
   and chopped
150 ml (¼ pint)
   Sancerre or other
   white wine
125 g (4 oz) button
   mushrooms,
   halved
chervil to garnish
   (optional)

Season the chicken breasts with salt and pepper to taste. Melt the butter in a heavy-based pan, add the bacon and cook for 2 to 3 minutes. Push to the side of the pan, add the chicken breasts and sauté for 4 to 5 minutes on each side. Add the wine and heat briskly for 2 to 3 minutes to evaporate the alcohol, then add the mushrooms. Cover and cook gently for 10 to 12 minutes.

Arrange on a bed of green noodles and garnish with chervil if wished. Serve with a tomato, onion and lettuce salad.
Serves 4

Chicken on Horseback

8 pitted prunes
4 chicken thighs
2 cloves garlic,
    crushed
8 rashers back bacon,
    derinded
2 teaspoons oil
6 tablespoons dry red
    wine

Open the prunes out flat. Rub the chicken thighs with the crushed garlic and press a prune on the top and bottom surfaces of each. Wrap a bacon rasher around each and secure with a wooden cocktail stick on the underside.

Brush with oil, place in a foil-lined pan, and cook towards the top of a preheated moderately hot oven, 200°C (400°F), Gas Mark 6, for 30 to 35 minutes; add the wine 15 minutes before the end of the cooking time.

Remove the cocktail sticks, arrange the chicken on a warmed serving dish and pour over the sauce. Serve hot, warm or cold, with a rice salad and mushrooms tossed with parsley.
Serves 4

Party Barbecue Drumsticks

12-16 chicken
    drumsticks
SAUCE:
3 tablespoons tomato
    ketchup
1 tablespoon oil
1 tablespoon cider
    vinegar
1 tablespoon soy
    sauce
2 tablespoons thick
    honey
2 teaspoons barbecue
    spice seasoning
1 teaspoon garlic salt
1 tablespoon onion
    powder
1 tablespoon paprika
1/2 teaspoon ground
    cinnamon
1/2 teaspoon ground
    cloves

Mix all the sauce ingredients together to form a smooth paste and use to coat the chicken drumsticks. Leave to stand for 30 minutes.

Oil the grill rack and arrange the drumsticks on it, without touching each other. Cook under a preheated moderately hot grill for 6 to 8 minutes on each side until tender, basting occasionally with extra paste, diluted with more cider vinegar if necessary.

Serve with coleslaw or green salad, tomato and cucumber vinaigrette and wholemeal bread.
Serves 6 to 8
NOTE: To cook on a barbecue, oil the grid and place about 10 cm (4 inches) above the coals. Cook for about 8 to 10 minutes on each side.

Stir-Fried Chicken Breasts

4 chicken breasts
2 tablespoons
    cornflour
2 tablespoons soya
    bean oil
1 teaspoon sesame oil
    (optional)
2 cloves garlic, finely
    chopped
1 × 250 g (8 oz) can
    sliced bamboo
    shoots, drained
150 ml (¼ pint)
    Chinese plum
    sauce
PANCAKES:
25 g (1 oz) plain
    flour
salt
2 eggs, beaten
150 ml (¼ pint)
    water
1 teaspoon brandy
1 tablespoon sesame
    oil
soya bean oil for
    frying
TO GARNISH:
4-8 spring onion fans
    (see page 27)
cucumber strips

First prepare the pancakes: sift the flour and salt into a bowl. Gradually add the eggs, beating until fairly smooth, then add the water, brandy and sesame oil.

Lightly oil a heavy-based pan and place over high heat until hot. Drop in 3 or 4 tablespoons batter, spacing them well apart, and cook, as separate small pancakes, until golden and bubbly. Turn and cook the other sides until golden. Repeat with the remaining batter. Stack the pancakes on a plate between sheets of greaseproof paper and keep warm over a pan of simmering water.

Skin and bone the chicken breasts and slice diagonally into thin slivers. Coat in the cornflour. Heat the oil(s) in a wok or frying pan, add the chicken in 2 or 3 batches and stir-fry for 3 minutes, pushing the chicken slivers to the side of the pan when cooked. Add the garlic, bamboo shoots and plum sauce. Stir gently and heat through until bubbling.

Transfer the chicken mixture to a warmed serving dish. Garnish with the spring onion fans and cucumber strips, and serve with the pancakes.
Serves 4

Chicken Wings Clamitano

16 chicken wings
284 ml (10 fl oz)
    can tomato and
    clam juice
3-4 shakes Tabasco
150 ml (¼ pint)
    water
2 bay leaves
12-16 black olives
salt and pepper
parsley sprigs to
    garnish

Put all the ingredients, except salt and pepper, into a pan and simmer, uncovered, for 35 minutes or until the chicken is very tender and the sauce has reduced slightly. Season with salt and pepper to taste, remembering to allow for the saltiness of the olives.

Garnish with parsley and serve with crisply cooked green beans.
Serves 4

Lymeswold Chicken Pots

150 ml (¼ pint)
  aspic
10-12 basil leaves
125 g (4 oz) cooked
  chicken, diced
75 g (3 oz)
  Lymeswold cheese
½ teaspoon celery
  salt
½ teaspoon paprika

Make up the aspic according to packet directions. Reserve 6 to 8 whole basil leaves and finely chop the remainder.

Using a food processor, electric blender or mincer, work the chicken, cheese, celery salt and paprika together until smooth. Blend in half the aspic and the chopped basil. Pour into small china pots or ramekins, smoothing the tops evenly, and press a reserved basil leaf into each. Pour over the remaining aspic. Chill until set.

Serve with toasted French bread and unsalted butter as a generous starter, or with a celery, pineapple and cress salad as a light lunch or supper dish.
Serves 6 to 8

Chicken with Pineapple

4 boneless chicken
  breasts
25 g (1 oz) butter
1 tablespoon olive oil
2 tablespoons dark
  rum, warmed
1 small pineapple,
  peeled and diced
1 tablespoon herb
  vinegar
15 g (½ oz) butter
TO GARNISH:
chicory leaves
parsley sprigs

Beat the chicken breasts to flatten
them slightly, then dry well on
kitchen paper.

Heat the butter and oil in a large,
shallow heavy-based pan, add the
chicken and sauté for 4 to 5 minutes
on each side, until golden. Add the
rum and carefully set alight. When
the flames die down, add half the
pineapple and the vinegar. Cook,
stirring frequently to dissolve all the
sediment, for 1 to 2 minutes.

Add the butter, tilting the pan to
mix, and continue cooking gently
until reduced to a smooth sauce.

Work the remaining pineapple in a
food processor or electric blender
until smooth.

Transfer the chicken and sauce to a
warmed serving dish and garnish
with chicory and parsley. Serve with
the puréed pineapple.

Serves 4

Steamed Chicken Creams

These unusual flavoured cream chicken mixtures make a pleasant starter, or light lunch or supper dish.

350 g (12 oz)
  boneless chicken
  breast, skinned and
  chopped
1/2 teaspoon salt
1/4 teaspoon ground
  white pepper
4 tablespoons dry
  vermouth
2 egg whites
142 ml (5 fl oz)
  double cream,
  lightly whipped
GARLIC AND
  MUSHROOM:
15 g (1/2 oz) butter
1 garlic clove, crushed
50 g (2 oz) flat
  mushrooms, diced
PRAWN AND DILL:
50 g (2 oz) cooked
  Pacific prawns,
  shelled and
  chopped
1 teaspoon chopped
  dill
SMOKED CHICKEN
  AND GHERKIN:
50 g (2 oz) cooked
  smoked chicken,
  diced
1 tablespoon diced
  gherkin
CHICKEN LIVER AND
  TOMATO:
2 teaspoons oil
2 chicken livers,
  halved and
  trimmed
1 teaspoon tomato
  purée

Put the chicken breast into a food processor or electric blender and work until smooth. Add the salt, pepper and vermouth and process again.

Whisk the egg whites to the soft foam stage and add to the chicken mixture. Process again briefly or stir until evenly blended.

Fold in the whipped cream and chill in the refrigerator while preparing the flavourings:

Garlic and Mushroom: Melt the butter in a small pan, add the garlic and mushrooms and sauté for 2 to 3 minutes. Stir into a quarter of the chicken cream mixture.

Prawn and Dill: Mix the prawns and dill together and stir into a quarter of the chicken cream mixture.

Smoked Chicken and Gherkin: Mix the smoked chicken and gherkin together and stir into a quarter of the chicken cream mixture.

Chicken Liver and Tomato: Heat the oil in a small pan, add the chicken livers and sauté for 2 minutes. Chop and mix with the tomato purée. Stir into a quarter of the chicken cream mixture.

To cook: Lightly oil four 150 ml (1/4 pint) ramekins, moulds or cups. Line the base of each with a piece of foil cut to fit exactly; oil again.

Spoon the mixtures into the containers, cover each with foil and place on a rack or trivet over 2 cm (3/4 inch) of boiling water in a saucepan, or place in a steamer. Cover securely and steam for 12 minutes or until firm.

Leave to cool for 1 minute then turn out, removing the foil. Slice each into 4 or 8.

To serve, arrange a few slices of each chicken cream on each individual plate, with a little shredded lettuce in the centre. Serve warm or cool, with Melba toast.

Serves 4

NOTE: If only one flavour is preferred, use 4 times the volume of one of the flavourings and proceed as above.

Giblet Rillettes

500 g (1 lb) chicken
  giblets
2 bay leaves
750 g (1½ lb) belly
  pork, diced
6 white peppercorns
6 cloves
2 cloves garlic,
  crushed
150 ml (¼ pint)
  water
2 tablespoons brandy
salt
paprika

Put all the ingredients, except the brandy, salt and paprika, in a casserole. Cover and cook in a preheated moderate oven, 180°C (350°F), Gas Mark 4, for about 3 hours, until very tender. Pour into a colander, reserving half the liquid. Discard the cloves and peppercorns and put the bay leaves on one side.

Strip as much meat from the neck bones as possible and cut away and discard the membrane from the gizzards. Bring the reserved liquid to the boil.

Put the meats into a food processor or electric blender with the boiling cooking liquid and the brandy and work to a semi-smooth purée. Add salt and paprika to taste.

Pour into a terrine or dish and press the reserved bay leaves on top. Chill until required.

Cut into thick slices and serve, as an inexpensive lunch or supper, with warm crusty bread, pickled onions and gherkins.

Serves 6 to 8
NOTE: This dish does not keep well and should be eaten within 2 days.

Creamy Chicken Livers Oporto

25 g (1 oz) butter
1 tablespoon oil
500 g (1 lb) chicken
  livers, trimmed
  and halved
3 celery sticks, sliced
4 tablespoons port
5 tablespoons soured
  cream
salt and pepper
celery leaves to
  garnish

Heat the butter and oil in a pan, add the livers and celery and sauté for 3 to 4 minutes, until the livers are golden outside but still pink inside. Add the port and simmer for a few minutes, until slightly reduced. Add the soured cream, tilting the pan to mix, and continue cooking gently until a smooth sauce forms. Season with salt and pepper to taste.

Garnish with celery leaves and serve with pasta tossed in a garlic-flavoured butter.

Serves 4

48

TURKEY, DUCK & GOOSE

Turkey Fillets Tonnato

4 × 125 g (4 oz)
  turkey breast fillets
salt and pepper
25 g (1 oz) butter
1 tablespoon olive oil
6 tablespoons medium
  dry white wine
1 × 198 g (7 oz) can
  tuna fish, drained
2 teaspoons tomato
  purée
150 g (5.2 oz)
  natural yogurt
TO GARNISH:
2 tablespoons
  chopped parsley
12 black olives
4 lemon wedges

Sprinkle the turkey fillets with salt and pepper to taste. Heat the butter and oil in a heavy-based frying pan, add the turkey and sauté for 3 to 4 minutes on each side, until well browned. Add the wine and cook gently for 2 to 3 minutes. Transfer the turkey to a warmed serving dish and keep hot.

Mash the tuna fish, tomato purée and a little of the yogurt together to form a creamy paste, then fold in the remaining yogurt. Pour into the pan, stirring well to blend, and heat through quickly. Spoon over the turkey, sprinkle with the parsley and garnish with the olives and lemon wedges.

Serve with green noodles.
Serves 4

Coconut Grove Turkey Steaks

15 g (½ oz) butter
1 tablespoon
    groundnut oil
4 × 125 g (4 oz)
    gammon-style
    turkey steaks
1 red pepper, cored,
    seeded and thinly
    sliced
150 ml (¼ pint)
    unsweetened
    pineapple juice
50 g (2 oz) creamed
    coconut, grated
2 tablespoons lemon
    or lime juice
salt
pinch of cayenne
    pepper
4 lemon or lime twists
    to garnish

Heat the butter and oil in a pan, add the turkey steaks and cook for 6 to 8 minutes, or according to packet directions. Transfer to a warmed serving dish and keep hot.

Add the red pepper to the pan and sauté for 1 minute. Add the pineapple juice, creamed coconut and lemon or lime juice, with salt and cayenne pepper to taste. Cook gently, stirring, until a creamy sauce forms.

Pour over the steaks and garnish with lemon or lime twists. Serve with mashed sweet potato and peas.
Serves 4

Thousand Island Turkey

25 g (1 oz) butter,
softened
1 tablespoon chopped
thyme
1 tablespoon lemon
juice
pinch of cayenne
pepper
4 × 125 g (4 oz)
turkey breast fillets
142 ml (5 fl oz)
whipping cream
2 tablespoons
Thousand Island
Dressing
TO SERVE:
shredded lettuce
tomato wedges

Place the butter in a bowl and beat in
the thyme, lemon juice and cayenne
until creamy. Spread over the turkey
fillets. Place in a foil-lined grill pan
and cook under a preheated moderate
grill for 10 to 12 minutes until tender,
turning halfway through cooking.
Transfer the turkey to a plate and
keep warm. Reserve the pan juices.

Whip the cream until soft but not
stiff, then fold in the pan juices and
Thousand Island Dressing.

Arrange the turkey on a bed of
lettuce and pour over a little sauce to
serve. Hand the rest separately.
Garnish with tomato wedges.
Serves 4

Thanksgiving Turkey with Pomegranate Sauce

1 × 5.5-7 kg
  (12-16 lb) turkey
  with giblets
sea salt
pepper
12-16 button onions
12-16 cloves
125 g (4 oz) unsalted
  butter, softened
  and diced
150 ml (¼ pint)
  water
300 ml (½ pint)
  white wine or cider
1 bay leaf
POMEGRANATE
  SAUCE:
1 pomegranate
50 g (2 oz) walnuts,
  chopped
finely grated rind and
  juice of 1 orange
  and 1 lemon
4 egg yolks
TO GARNISH:
herb sprigs

Set aside the turkey giblets. Season the cavity of the turkey with sea salt and pepper. Stud each onion with a clove and use these and half the butter to fill the cavity. Truss the turkey securely* and spread with the remaining butter.

Chop the giblets and place in a roasting pan with the water, wine or cider, and bay leaf. Place the turkey in the pan and cover loosely with foil. Cook in a preheated moderately hot oven, 190°C (375°F), Gas Mark 5, for 15 minutes per pound or until the juices run clear yellow*; remove the foil for the last 30 minutes. Transfer to a warmed serving dish and keep warm. Strain the cooking juices and reserve.

To make the pomegranate sauce, cut the pomegranate in half crossways and extract the juice with a lemon squeezer. Add the walnuts, orange and lemon rind and juice, and reserved cooking juices to make up to 600 ml (1 pint). Pour into a saucepan and simmer gently.

Lightly whisk the egg yolks in a separate bowl, gradually adding 5 to 6 tablespoons of the pomegranate sauce. Remove the pan from the heat, tip in the egg yolk mixture and whisk well; *do not reheat.*

To serve, garnish the turkey with herbs and surround with sautéed potatoes and buttered carrots. Serve a clove-studded onion with each portion and hand the sauce separately.
Serves 12 to 16

Turkey Wings in Oyster Sauce

6 prime turkey
  wings
1 tablespoon light
  soy sauce
450 ml (¾ pint)
  turkey stock* or
  water
4 tablespoons chilli
  vinegar
25 g (1 oz) root
  ginger, roughly
  sliced
1 clove garlic,
  crushed
1 teaspoon dill seeds
6 tablespoons oyster
  sauce
4 spring onions,
  sliced
TO GARNISH:
4 spring onion fans
  (see page 27)

Put the turkey wings, soy sauce, stock or water, vinegar, ginger, garlic and dill seeds in a large pan. Cover and simmer for 50 to 55 minutes or until tender. Transfer the turkey to a warmed serving dish and keep hot.

Strain the cooking liquid. Measure 4 tablespoons and add to the pan with the oyster sauce and spring onions and bring to the boil. Slice the turkey off the bones and arrange on a bed of noodles. Pour over the sauce and garnish with spring onion fans.
Serves 6

Boned Turkey Extravaganza

1 × 7 kg (16 lb)
  turkey, boned*
salt and pepper
750 g (1½ lb) young
  spinach leaves,
  stalks removed
1 kg (2 lb) piece
  gammon, derinded
  and cubed
750 g (1½ lb)
  chicken livers,
  trimmed and
  halved
2 pawpaws, peeled,
  seeded and sliced
50 g (2 oz) butter,
  softened
parsley to garnish

Place the turkey, skin side down, on oiled heavy-duty cooking foil and sprinkle liberally with salt and pepper. Cover with the spinach, stuffing carefully into the leg cavities. Place a row of gammon down the centre and arrange the chicken livers on both sides. Cover with pawpaw.

Overlap the turkey edges. Secure with skewers and string. Tie extra string around the turkey, crossing over the breast. Turn right way up.

Carefully lift the turkey, on its foil, into a roasting pan and spread with the butter. Cook in a preheated moderate oven, 160°C (325°F), Gas Mark 3, for 3¾ hours or until the juices run clear yellow*, basting every 30 minutes.

Leave the turkey to stand for 15 minutes. Skim off the excess fat from the pan juices and make gravy*.

Remove the string and skewers and carve the turkey crossways. Garnish with parsley. Serve with the gravy.
Serves 12 to 16

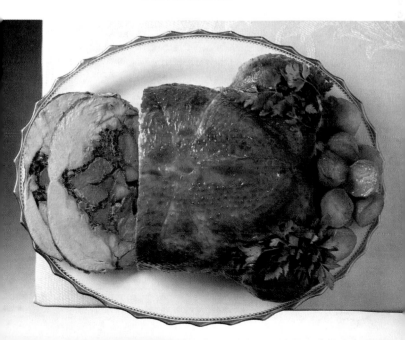

Self-Basting Turkey with Lemon Stuffing

1 × 4.5-5 kg
  (10-11 lb) self-
  basting turkey
1 tablespoon plain
  flour
150 ml (¼ pint) red
  wine
150 ml (¼ pint)
  water
salt and pepper
LEMON STUFFING:
1 lemon
1 large Granny
  Smith or Golden
  Delicious apple
4 rashers back bacon,
  derinded and
  chopped
4 marjoram sprigs
2 sage leaves,
  chopped
¼ teaspoon pepper
CHESTNUT
  STUFFING:
1 × 75 g (3 oz)
  packet chestnut
  stuffing mix
125 g (4 oz) pre-
  soaked dried
  apricots, chopped
15 g (½ oz) chopped
  suet or butter
TO GARNISH:
herb sprigs

First make the lemon stuffing. Finely grate the rind from the lemon, remove and discard the pith and chop the lemon flesh very finely. Quarter, core and chop the apple and mix thoroughly with the lemon rind and flesh, bacon, marjoram, sage and pepper.

Fill the neck cavity of the turkey with the lemon stuffing, securing underneath with wooden cocktail sticks. Truss the turkey securely*. Place in a roasting pan and cook in a preheated moderate oven, 180°C (350°F), Gas Mark 4, for 3 to 3½ hours, or 3¼ to 3¾ hours if foil covered, until the juices run clear yellow*.

Make up the chestnut stuffing following the packet directions, adding the apricots and suet or butter. Roll into small balls and place around the turkey 30 minutes before the end of cooking time.

Transfer the turkey to a warmed serving dish with the stuffing balls and keep warm.

Pour off all but 1 tablespoon of fat from the pan. Add the flour to the pan and cook on top of the stove, stirring, until bubbling. Gradually blend in the wine and water and cook, stirring, until smooth. Add salt and pepper to taste.

Garnish the turkey with herbs and serve with courgettes, baked tomatoes and potatoes. Hand the sauce separately.

Serves 10 to 12

Turkey Breasts Colombian

2 × 250 g (8 oz)
   turkey breast fillets
salt and pepper
25 g (1 oz) butter
2 tablespoons olive
   oil
1 lemon, halved
SAUCE:
1 avocado, peeled,
   stoned and cubed
4 spring onions,
   sliced
½ green pepper,
   cored, seeded and
   cubed
3 drops Tabasco
   sauce
142 ml (5 fl oz)
   soured cream
TO GARNISH:
½ green pepper,
   cored, seeded and
   sliced into rings

Holding the turkey fillets firmly and using a sharp knife, cut through horizontally to give 4 thin slices. Place in one layer between 2 sheets of waxed paper and beat with a rolling pine or wooden mallet to flatten. Season liberally with salt and pepper.

Heat the butter and oil in a pan. Add the fillets, two at a time, and sauté for 2 minutes on each side. Return all fillets to the pan, lower the heat, squeeze over the juice from ½ lemon and keep warm.

To make the sauce, mash the avocado to a paste with the juice of the remaining lemon half. Add the spring onions, green pepper, Tabasco, and salt to taste, then fold in the cream.

Arrange the turkey on a warmed serving dish and trickle over the sauce. Garnish with the pepper rings.
Serves 4

57

Sweet-Sour Turkey Sausages

500 g (1 lb) turkey sausages
SWEET–SOUR SAUCE:
25 g (1 oz) butter
1 onion, chopped
2 celery sticks, diagonally sliced
1 dessert apple, peeled, cored and cut into segments
25 g (1 oz) preserved ginger, drained and sliced
2 tablespoons ginger syrup
1 × 439 g (15½ oz) can pineapple pieces in unsweetened juice
1 tablespoon cornflour
2 tablespoons water
TO GARNISH:
celery leaves

Fry the sausages in a non-stick or lightly oiled pan over low heat for 20 minutes or until cooked.

Meanwhile, prepare the sauce. Melt the butter in a small pan, add the onion, celery and apple and sauté until barely tender. Add the ginger, ginger syrup and pineapple with its juice and simmer for 5 minutes. Blend the cornflour with the water and add to the sauce, stirring until thickened, then simmer for 2 minutes.

Drain the sausages on kitchen paper, place on a warmed serving dish and spoon over the hot sauce. Garnish with celery leaves and serve with rice or noodles and peas.
Serves 4

Scrambled Turkey Livers with Basil

This makes a delicious brunch, lunch or supper party dish served with chilled Chablis and followed by a mixed salad.

6 eggs
2 tablespoons double cream
salt and pepper
50 g (2 oz) butter
2 × 227 g (8 oz) cartons frozen turkey livers, thawed, trimmed and quartered
6-8 basil leaves
8 thin slices French bread, toasted

Place the eggs and cream in a small bowl with salt and pepper to taste and beat lightly with a fork.

Melt half the butter in a small frying pan, add the livers and sauté briskly until golden on the outside but still pink inside. Turn the heat to very low.

Melt the remaining butter in another pan until foaming, add the eggs and scramble until creamy, stirring only enough to prevent sticking. Pile the egg onto a warmed serving dish and spoon the livers on top. Chop half the basil and sprinkle over all.

Garnish with the remaining basil and serve immediately with the toast.
Serves 4

Turkey Mince Roulade

1 kg (2 lb) raw
   turkey, minced
½ teaspoon garlic salt
½ teaspoon pepper
1 onion, coarsely
   grated
6 slices cooked ham
250 g (8 oz) carrot,
   grated
2 red peppers, cored,
   seeded and diced
50 g (2 oz) raisins
75 g (3 oz)
   hazelnuts, coarsely
   chopped
1 teaspoon soy sauce
DRESSING:
½ teaspoon turmeric
½ teaspoon cumin
½ teaspoon paprika
6 tablespoons
   mayonnaise
4 tablespoons natural
   yogurt

Mix the turkey, garlic salt, pepper
and onion together until smooth.
With dampened hands, smooth out
the mixture on oiled foil to form a
rectangle 25 × 35 cm (10 × 15 inches).
Cover with the ham, overlapping the
slices if necessary. Spread the carrot,
red pepper, raisins and nuts over the
ham.

Lifting one side of the foil, roll up
the meat tightly, finishing with the
join underneath. Pinch the ends
together tightly to seal. Place on a
baking sheet and cook in a preheated
moderate oven, 180°C (350°F), Gas
Mark 4, for 20 minutes.

Open the foil, brush the roulade
with the soy sauce and return to the
oven for 30 minutes.

Mix the dressing ingredients
together. Cut the roulade into thick
slices. Spoon over the dressing and
serve cold with salad. Alternatively,
serve hot with the pan juices, handed
separately.
Serves 4 to 6

Turkey with Apricots

300 ml (½ pint)
  milk
2 small onions,
  quartered
1 bay leaf
1 parsley sprig
pinch of ground mace
4 white peppercorns
25 g (1 oz) butter
2 tablespoons plain
  flour
salt
1 × 411 g (14½ oz)
  can apricot halves
625 g (1¼ lb) cooked
  turkey, diced
2 tablespoons grated
  Parmesan cheese
25 g (1 oz) flaked
  almonds

Put the milk, onions, bay leaf, parsley, mace and peppercorns in a small pan and simmer, uncovered, for 2 minutes. Turn off the heat and leave for 10 minutes for the flavours to infuse, then strain and set aside.

Melt the butter in a pan, stir in the flour and salt to taste and cook for 1 minute. Gradually add the reserved milk, stirring until smooth. Drain the apricots and add 2 tablespoons of the juice to the sauce; cook for 2 to 3 minutes. Stir in the turkey and remove from the heat.

Oil an ovenproof serving dish or casserole and fill with the turkey mixture. Tuck in apricot halves at intervals. Scatter the Parmesan and almonds over the top. Cook in a preheated moderate oven, 180°C (350°F), Gas Mark 4, for 15 minutes. Increase the heat to 220°C (425°F), Gas Mark 7, and cook for 5 minutes to brown the top.

Serve with plain boiled rice.
Serves 4 to 6

Marinated Grilled Duck

4 duck breast and
    wing portions
MARINADE:
1 teaspoon soy sauce
150 ml (¼ pint) red
    wine vinegar
1 onion, chopped
12 juniper berries,
    crushed
2 teaspoons fennel
    seeds
1 clove garlic, crushed
SAUCE:
150 g (5.2 oz)
    natural yogurt
salt and pepper
TO GARNISH:
watercress sprigs

Put the duck portions in a large clear plastic bag. Add marinade ingredients, exclude any air and seal. Leave for 8 hours, turning occasionally.

Drain, reserving the marinade, and place, skin side down, in a roasting pan. Cook in a preheated hot oven, 220°C (425°F), Gas Mark 7, for 30 minutes, basting once with the marinade. Turn and cook for a further 30 minutes, basting again. Transfer to a warmed dish; keep hot.

Place 6 tablespoons of the reserved marinade in a small pan, cover and heat gently for 5 minutes. Strain, whisk into the yogurt and season with salt and pepper to taste.

Serve the duck on a bed of brown rice, garnished with watercress and topped with the sauce.
Serves 4

Caramel Duck with Limes

1 dessert apple
1 grapefruit,
  segmented
1 teaspoon Cointreau
4 duck breast and
  wing portions
sea salt
pepper
2 tablespoons clear
  honey
15 g (½ oz) butter
15 g (½ oz) olive oil
  or rendered duck
  fat*
2 tablespoons caster
  sugar
shredded rind and
  juice of 2 limes

Peel and core the apple and cut into cubes, or scoop into balls using a melon baller. Place the apple, grapefruit and Cointreau in a basin and leave to stand for 30 minutes.

Cut the meat from each duck breast, in one piece; keep the bones and wings for stock, if liked. Press salt and pepper to taste into both sides of the flesh and spread with the honey.

Heat the butter and oil or fat in a heavy-based pan, add the duck and cook for 4 to 5 minutes on each side or until the juices run barely pink, pressing down firmly to prevent curling. Remove from the pan and keep hot.

Pour off the pan juices and set aside. Add the sugar to the pan and heat, without stirring, until it caramelizes. Remove from the heat and add the lime juice and reserved pan juices. Stir over a low heat until a smooth sauce forms, adding a little water if it becomes too thick. Add half the lime rind and continue cooking over very low heat while preparing the garnish.

Drain the grapefruit segments and apple pieces and arrange in a fan shape at one side of the serving dish. Pour the caramel sauce into the centre of the dish.

Slice each duck breast through 6 or 7 times diagonally, keeping the meat in its correct shape. Arrange on the serving dish spreading the slices a little to give a striped effect.

Serve with a celeriac purée* and a chicory and watercress salad if wished.

Serves 4

Llanover Duckling

1 × 1.75 kg (4 lb)
  duckling with
  giblets
300 ml (½ pint) dry
  white wine
450 ml (¾ pint)
  water
450 ml (¾ pint)
  medium dry cider
bunch of mixed
  parsley, thyme,
  bay leaf and sage
1 leek, white part
  only, shredded
4 tablespoons single
  cream
1 tablespoon chopped
  parsley
pepper
BRINE SOLUTION:
25 g (1 oz) saltpetre
350 g (12 oz) sea salt
250 g (8 oz) soft
  brown sugar
600 ml (1 pint)
  boiling water
1.75 litres (3 pints)
  cold water
TO SERVE:
½ head of curly
  endive
2 kiwi fruit, peeled
  and sliced
1 Ogen melon,
  peeled, seeded and
  segmented
few bay leaves
  (optional)

Remove the giblets from the duck and set aside. Prepare the brine solution: put the saltpetre, sea salt and sugar in a large non-metal bowl, pour over the boiling water and stir until dissolved. Add the cold water and the duck. Cover and leave in the refrigerator for 2 days.

Discard the brine solution, wash the duck thoroughly and dry well; truss securely*. Place in a large flameproof casserole with the wine, water, 300 ml (½ pint) of the cider, giblets (except the liver) and herbs. Bring to simmering point, cover and cook gently for 1 hour or until tender. Remove the duck and keep hot.

Strain off 150 ml (¼ pint) of the cooking juices and add the remaining cider, the leek and the reserved liver. Bring to the boil and boil rapidly for 8 minutes, until reduced by half. Place in a food processor or electric blender and work to a purée. Stir in the cream, parsley, and pepper to taste.

Arrange the endive, kiwi fruit and melon on a large serving dish. Lift the duck into the centre and pour over a little sauce; serve the rest separately. Garnish with bay leaves if wished. Cut the duck into wafer-thin slices to serve.

Serves 4

NOTE: Saltpetre is available from most chemists.

Roast Duck with Ginger Wine

1 × 2 kg (4½ lb)
  duck
salt and pepper
8 bay leaves, lightly
  crushed
4 tablespoons ginger
  wine
SAUCE:
1 cooking apple,
  peeled, cored and
  diced
3 tablespoons ginger
  wine
1 tablespoon clear
  honey

Sprinkle the duck inside and out with salt and pepper and put the bay leaves in the cavity. Truss securely*, prick the duck all over and brush with the ginger wine. Place on a rack in a roasting pan, cover loosely with foil and cook in a preheated moderately hot oven, 200°C (400°F), Gas Mark 6, for 45 minutes.

Remove the foil, pour off the fat from the pan and reserve 1 tablespoon. Return the duck to the oven and cook for a further 45 minutes or until tender. Transfer to a warmed serving dish and keep warm.

To make the sauce, put the reserved fat, the apple and ginger wine in a pan, cover and simmer for 12 minutes, then stir in the honey. Purée in a food processor or electric blender, or beat with a fork. Serve with the duck.

Serves 4

Fionnuala's Ducklings

2 × 1.75 kg (4 lb)
  ducklings
salt and pepper
250 g (8 oz) young
  turnips, quartered
  and parboiled
125 g (4 oz) shallots,
  parboiled
250 g (8 oz) young
  carrots, halved
  lengthways and
  parboiled
4 winter savory
  sprigs
150 ml (¼ pint)
  stock
150 ml (¼ pint)
  white burgundy
2 × 397 g (14 oz)
  cans petit pois,
  drained
2 teaspoons cornflour,
  blended with
  1 tablespoon water
6 tablespoons extra
  thick cream

Prick the ducks all over and season
inside and out with salt and pepper.
Truss securely*, place on a rack in a
roasting pan and cook in a preheated
hot oven, 220°C (425°F), Gas Mark 7,
for 45 minutes or until golden.

Lower the temperature to 200°C
(400°F), Gas Mark 6. Remove rack,
drain off the fat and put the ducks in
the pan. Add the turnips, shallots,
carrots, savory, stock and wine.
Cover loosely with foil and cook for
45 minutes. Remove foil. Add the
peas and heat through for 10 minutes.

Transfer the ducks to a warmed
serving dish and surround with the
vegetables; keep warm. Pour the
cooking liquid into a clean pan and
boil rapidly for 5 minutes. Season to
taste with salt and pepper. Add the
blended cornflour and cook, stirring,
until smooth and thickened, then stir
in the cream. Pour over the
vegetables and serve immediately.
Serves 6

Braised Williamsburg Goose

1 × 5 kg (11 lb)
  oven-ready goose
6-8 dessert apples,
  peeled and cored
12-16 stoned dates
salt and pepper
2 celery sticks,
  chopped
150 ml (¼ pint) red
  wine
150 ml (¼ pint)
  water
150 ml (¼ pint) red
  wine vinegar
4 marjoram sprigs
2 teaspoons powdered
  bay
1 bunch spring
  onions, tied with
  string
3-4 pears, peeled,
  halved and cored
4 tablespoons
  redcurrant jelly
parsley to garnish

Remove all visible fat from the cavity of the goose and prick the skin of the lower breast and legs. Stuff each apple with 2 dates and use to fill the body cavity. Truss the goose securely*, season liberally with salt and pepper and place on a rack in a roasting pan. Add the celery to the pan, then pour in the wine and water. Cook in a preheated moderately hot oven, 200°C (400°F), Gas Mark 6, for 1½ hours, basting occasionally. Lower the temperature to 180°C (350°F), Gas Mark 4.

Set the goose aside and pour off the pan juices. Return the goose to the pan without the rack. Add the vinegar, marjoram, bay, spring onions and pears. Cover loosely with foil and return to the oven for 1¾ to 2 hours, or until a meat thermometer inserted into the leg registers 88°C (190°F).

Transfer the goose and half the pears to a warmed serving dish and keep warm.

Drain the remaining pears and spring onions (removing the string) and place in a food processor, electric blender or sieve. Pour the liquid from the roasting pan into a measuring jug and remove the fat. Add the liquid to the pears and onions and work to a purée. Return to the pan with the redcurrant jelly and boil rapidly until reduced and syrupy.

Garnish the goose with parsley. Serve with roast potatoes or celeriac and broccoli, serving an apple from inside the goose and a pear half with each portion. Hand the sauce separately.
Serves 6 to 8

Celebration Roast Goose

4.5-5 kg (10-11 lb)
   goose with giblets
STUFFING:
1 × 435 g (1 lb) can
   chestnut purée
350 g (12 oz)
   potatoes, boiled
   and mashed
8 rashers back bacon,
   derinded and
   chopped
1 tablespoon chopped
   lemon thyme
1 tablespoon chopped
   sage
finely grated rind of
   1 lemon
SAUCE:
25 g (1 oz) butter
1 large onion,
   chopped
250 g (8 oz) sharp-
   flavoured dessert
   apples, peeled,
   cored and chopped
1 tablespoon clear
   honey
juice of 1 lemon
½ teaspoon powdered
   cardamom
salt

Remove the giblets and set aside, chopping the liver. Remove all visible fat from the cavity of the goose and prick the skin of the lower breast and legs well.

Mix the stuffing ingredients together well, adding the chopped goose liver, and pepper to taste. Use to fill the cavity. Truss the goose firmly*, securing the vent with string.

Put the remaining giblets in a roasting pan. Place a rack in the pan and put the goose on top. Pour in 300 ml (½ pint) water.

Cover loosely with foil and cook in a preheated moderately hot oven, 190°C (375°F), Gas Mark 5, for 30 minutes, then lower the temperature to 180°C (350°F), Gas Mark 4. Cook for 3¼ to 3¾ hours, until the juices run clear yellow* and a meat thermometer inserted into the leg registers 88°C (190°F); baste occasionally with the liquid and add more water if necessary. Remove the foil after 3 hours to allow the skin to become golden and crisp. Transfer to a warmed serving dish and keep hot.

To make the sauce, melt the butter in a pan and add the onion, apple, honey and lemon juice. Cover and cook for about 12 to 15 minutes, until the onion is soft, then add the cardamom, and salt and pepper to taste. Using a food processor or electric blender, work to a smooth sauce, or rub through a sieve; if a rougher texture is preferred mash with a fork.

Serve the goose accompanied by leek rings and buttered carrot strips. Hand the sauce separately.
Serves 6 to 8

FEATHERED GAME

Classic Grouse Casserole

2 oven-ready
  casserole grouse
salt and pepper
1 small onion,
  chopped
40 g (1½ oz) butter
1 teaspoon thyme
  leaves
2 juniper berries,
  crushed
150 ml (¼ pint)
  game stock* or dry
  cider
2 tablespoons guava,
  cranberry or
  rowanberry jelly

Season the grouse inside and out with salt and pepper and place half the onion inside each body cavity. Mix the butter, thyme and juniper berries together and spread all over the grouse. Place in a roasting pan and cook in a preheated moderate oven, 180°C (350°F), Gas Mark 4, for 20 minutes.

Cut the grouse in half lengthways and place in a casserole dish. Add the stock or cider and jelly, cover and return to the oven for 30 minutes.

Serve with carrot purée* and leeks.
Serves 2

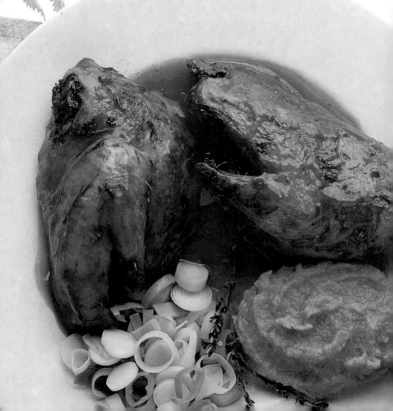

Grouse with Rum Butter

2 oven-ready young grouse
salt
pinch of cayenne pepper
15 g (½ oz) butter
2 lovage sprigs or a few celery leaves
4 rashers streaky bacon, derinded

RUM BUTTER:
1 tablespoon dark rum
25 g (1 oz) butter, softened

TO GARNISH:
2 slices of toast, cut into rounds
lovage sprigs or celery leaves
chicory leaves

Season the grouse inside and out with salt and cayenne. Put half the butter and a lovage sprig or celery leaves inside each body cavity. Wrap 2 bacon rashers around each grouse, securing underneath with a wooden cocktail stick, and place in a roasting pan. Cook in a preheated hot oven, 220°C (425°F), Gas Mark 7, for 15 to 20 minutes, basting once.

Blend the rum into the butter. Remove the bacon from the grouse and set aside. Return the grouse to the pan and baste with the rum butter. Cook for a further 15 minutes, until the breasts are browned and the flesh is pink but not raw. Put a slice of toast under each grouse for the last 5 minutes to absorb the juices.

Serve the grouse on the toast, spoon over the buttery juices and garnish with the bacon, lovage or celery leaves, and chicory. Serve with blackberry jelly.
Serves 2

Boursin Pheasant

1 brace of oven-ready
    pheasant
salt and pepper
15 g (½ oz) butter
1 tablespoon olive oil
50 g (2 oz) pine nuts
125 g (4 oz) Boursin
    cheese
125 g (4 oz) dried
    apricots, finely
    sliced
4 rashers back bacon,
    derinded
4 tablespoons game
    stock*
watercress to garnish

Sprinkle the pheasants inside and out with salt and pepper. Heat the butter and oil in a roasting pan, add the pheasants and cook for 10 minutes, until browned all over. Remove from the pan and cool slightly.

Add the pine nuts to the pan and cook until golden. Remove with a slotted spoon and set aside one third. Put the remaining nuts, the Boursin and apricots into the pheasant cavities, dividing equally. Lay 2 bacon rashers across each breast and truss securely. Cook in a preheated moderately hot oven, 190°C (375°F), Gas Mark 5, for 40 to 45 minutes.

Transfer the pheasants to a warmed serving dish and spoon the reserved nuts around them. Pour off all but 1 tablespoon of fat from the pan. Pour in the stock and heat, stirring, to dissolve the sediment. Pour over the pheasants. Garnish with watercress. Serve with sautéed celeriac.
Serves 4 to 6

Polish Pheasant

2 oven-ready hen
    pheasant
salt and pepper
250 g (8 oz) Bozcek,
    derinded and cubed
    (see note)
3 tablespoons gin
1 × 1 kg (2 lb) jar or
    can sauerkraut,
    drained
150 ml (¼ pint) dry
    white wine
½ teaspoon caraway
    seeds
6 juniper berries
SAUCE:
350 g (12 oz)
    damsons or other
    plums, stoned and
    sliced
1 tablespoon gin
1 tablespoon plum
    jelly or jam

Season pheasants inside and out with salt and pepper. Cook the Bozcek in a large flameproof casserole over moderate heat until the fat runs. Add the pheasants and cook for 10 minutes, until browned. Remove the pheasants and Bozcek and set aside.

Add the gin to the pan and stir to dissolve the sediment. Add the sauerkraut, wine, caraway seeds and juniper berries. Replace pheasants, covering the breasts with the Bozcek. Cover and cook in a preheated moderately hot oven, 200°C (400°F), Gas Mark 6, for 45 to 50 minutes.

Meanwhile, make the sauce. Cook the damsons with the gin and plum jelly for 8 to 10 minutes, until soft. Work in a food processor or electric blender until smooth. Serve the sauce with the pheasants and sauerkraut.
Serves 4 to 6

NOTE: Bozcek is Polish smoked lean belly of pork. Smoked streaky bacon can be used as a substitute.

Pigeons from Béarn

50 g (2 oz) butter
1 tablespoon olive oil
2 oven-ready wood
    pigeons
350 g (12 oz)
    Jerusalem
    artichokes or
    artichoke hearts,
    cooked and diced
cayenne pepper
MARINADE:
juice of 1 lemon
2 tablespoons white
    wine
4 tablespoons brandy
salt and pepper
TO GARNISH:
lemon slices
parsley sprigs

Heat half the butter and the oil in a pan, add the pigeons and cook gently for 5 minutes, until brown on all sides. Cover the pan and cook over low heat for 30 to 35 minutes, until tender. Remove the pigeons with a slotted spoon, reserving the fat left in the pan.

Using a sharp knife or poultry shears, halve the pigeons lengthways and place cut side down in a shallow non-metal dish. Pour over the lemon juice, wine, brandy, and salt and pepper to taste and leave to marinate in a warm place for 15 minutes.

Meanwhile, melt the remaining butter in the pan, add the artichokes and sauté for 2 to 3 minutes, seasoning with salt and cayenne to taste. Place in a food processor or electric blender and work to a purée, or rub through a sieve. Mound the artichoke purée on an ovenproof serving dish, hollowing slightly.

Remove the pigeons from the marinade with a slotted spoon and set aside. Place the marinade in a small pan and heat through gently for 5 minutes.

Scrape out the residue from inside the pigeons and add to the marinade with the reserved cooking fat. Stir thoroughly, then pour into the hollow of the artichoke purée. Lay the pigeons on top. Place in a preheated moderately hot oven, 190°C (375°F), Gas Mark 5, for 5 minutes to heat through thoroughly.

Serve the pigeons immediately, garnished with lemon slices and parsley.
Serves 2

Mallard Mercedes

2 oven-ready mallard
salt and pepper
1 shallot or small
    onion, finely
    chopped
grated rind and juice
    of 1 orange
2 tablespoons orange
    shred marmalade
6 tablespoons port
TO GARNISH:
orange twists
fried white
    breadcrumbs
watercress sprigs

Sprinkle the mallard inside and out with salt and pepper. Put half the shallot or onion in each body cavity. Spread the orange rind over the mallard and place in a small roasting pan. Cook in a preheated moderately hot oven, 200°C (400°F), Gas Mark 6, for 20 minutes, basting twice.

Warm the marmalade with the port in a small pan until dissolved. Spoon off half the fat from the roasting pan and pour the port mixture over the mallard. Return to the oven for 20 to 25 minutes, basting occasionally.

Transfer the mallard to a warmed serving dish; keep warm. Skim off as much fat as possible from the pan, add the orange juice and cook on top of the stove, stirring, until the sauce is smooth.

Pour the sauce over the mallard and garnish with orange twists, fried breadcrumbs and watercress to serve.
Serves 4 to 6

Pigeons in Honey

1 teaspoon coriander
   seeds, lightly
   crushed
2 tablespoons honey
2 onions, sliced
300 ml (½ pint) dry
   cider
300 ml (½ pint)
   chilli vinegar
4 oven-ready wood
   pigeons, halved
   lengthwise
salt and pepper
25 g (1 oz) butter
2 tablespoons oil
chopped parsley to
   garnish

Mix the coriander, honey, onion,
cider and vinegar in a large non-metal
bowl. Add the pigeons and leave to
marinate for 8 hours or overnight.
Drain, reserving marinade; dry well.

Heat the butter and oil in a large
flameproof casserole, add the pigeons
in 2 batches, seasoning them with salt
and pepper, and brown on both sides.
Put all the birds in the casserole and
pour over the marinade. Cover and
cook in a preheated moderate oven,
160°C (325°F), Gas Mark 3, for 1 to
1¼ hours, until tender.

Serve garnished with parsley, and
accompanied by sautéed mushrooms
and a celery julienne.

Serves 4

Quails Bianco

125 g (4 oz) butter
8 quails
pepper
4 slices Parma or
 other raw smoked
 ham, halved
 crossways
10 fresh or preserved
 vine leaves,
 blanched
3 fresh figs, quartered
4 tablespoons rosé
 wine
150 ml (¼ pint)
 Bianco vermouth

Spread half the butter all over the quails, then sprinkle with pepper. Wrap a half slice of ham over the breast of each quail, securing underneath with a wooden cocktail stick. Place each quail on a vine leaf. Shred the 2 remaining leaves.

Generously coat the inside of a shallow ovenproof serving dish with the remaining butter. Place the quails, on the leaves, in the dish, arranging the shredded leaves and the fig segments near the centre. Pour over the wine and vermouth. Cook in a preheated moderate oven, 180°C (350°F), Gas Mark 4, for 40 to 45 minutes, basting occasionally.

Serve with a julienne of celery, courgette and carrot.
Serves 4

Roast Pigeons Paloma

50 g (2 oz) butter,
 softened
1 teaspoon chopped
 parsley
1 teaspoon chopped
 lemon balm
 (optional)
1 teaspoon chopped
 chives
2 shakes of Tabasco
2 oven-ready wood
 pigeons
2 × 7.5 cm (3 inch)
 wide sheets pork
 barding fat, thinly
 sliced
1 teaspoon plain flour
1 tablespoon lemon
 juice
TO GARNISH:
lemon balm or
 parsley
small bunch of grapes

Blend the butter with the herbs and Tabasco and put half the mixture inside the body cavity of each pigeon. Wrap each pigeon in a piece of pork fat and truss, bringing the trussing strings across the breast to secure firmly.

Place the pigeons in a roasting pan and cook in a preheated moderately hot oven, 200°C (400°F), Gas Mark 6, for 20 to 25 minutes, basting twice.

Remove the barding fat, sprinkle the breasts with the flour, baste again and return to the oven for 5 minutes, until golden. Pour the lemon juice into the pan, stirring to dissolve the sediment, then spoon over the pigeons.

Transfer to a warmed serving dish and garnish with lemon balm or parsley and grapes. Serve with game chips*.
Serves 2

Partridge with Quince

2 oven-ready young
    partridges
salt and pepper
2 teaspoons butter
2 cloves garlic
2 parsley sprigs
4 rashers streaky
    bacon, derinded
1 ripe quince, peeled,
    cored and cut into 8
150 ml (¼ pint) dry
    vermouth
1 teaspoon cornflour
4 tablespoons double
    cream
1 bunch watercress to
    garnish

Season the partridges inside and out with salt and pepper. Put 1 teaspoon butter, 1 garlic clove and a parsley sprig inside each body cavity. Wrap 2 bacon rashers around each partridge, securing underneath with wooden cocktail sticks. Place in a roasting pan and cook in a preheated hot oven, 220°C (425°F), Gas Mark 7, for 15 minutes. Add the quince, turning to coat in the pan juices, and return to the oven for 20 minutes, or until the partridges are tender. Transfer the partridges and quince to a warmed serving dish; keep hot.

Pour the vermouth into the pan and stir well to dissolve the sediment. Stir the cornflour into a little of the cream, add the remaining cream, then pour into the pan. Cook gently, stirring, for 2 to 3 minutes until smooth and thickened.

Garnish the partridges with watercress. Serve with the sauce.
Serves 2

Spit-Roast Partridge

2 oven-ready young
    partridges
salt and pepper
2 rashers streaky
    bacon, derinded
    and chopped
4 juniper berries,
    crushed
25 g (1 oz) butter
1 teaspoon Pernod or
    other aromatic
    liqueur
TO GARNISH:
chopped parsley
radicchio or lettuce
    leaves

Season the partridges inside and out with salt and pepper. Fry the bacon in its own fat for 3 to 4 minutes; reserve the fat. Place half the bacon inside each body cavity and truss securely. Mix the juniper berries, butter and Pernod together and spread over the partridges.

Secure the partridges firmly on the rotisserie skewer, keeping them in place with the two–pronged 'forks' at either end. Turn on the rotisserie and check the partridges are centred well. Cook for 15 minutes on a high heat and 15 minutes on a low heat, basting with the reserved bacon fat and the juices in the rotisserie pan.

Transfer the partridges to a warmed serving dish and leave to stand for 2 to 3 minutes. Sprinkle with parsley and garnish with radicchio or lettuce leaves. Serve with small triangles of toast, spread with pan dripping.
Serves 2

Salmis of Partridge

2 slices Parma or raw
    smoked ham,
    halved
2 oven-ready
    partridges
pepper
1 tablespoon olive oil
40 g (1½ oz) butter
4 shallots or 1 small
    onion, chopped
bunch of mixed
    parsley, thyme and
    winter savory
4 tablespoons game
    stock* or water
6 tablespoons red
    wine
2 tablespoons port
TO GARNISH:
watercress sprigs
2 slices bread, toasted
    and cut into
    triangles

Place a half ham slice in the cavity of each partridge. Sprinkle with pepper and truss securely.

Heat the oil and butter in a frying pan, add the partridges and fry for 15 to 20 minutes, until browned. Remove from the pan; cool slightly.

Using a sharp knife or poultry shears, cut off and reserve the wing, leg and breast portions. Cut up the carcasses and put in a saucepan with the shallots or onion and herbs.

Pour the stock or water into the frying pan and stir well to dissolve the sediment. Add to the saucepan with the wine. Cover and cook gently for 1 hour. Strain, then add the port.

Shred the remaining ham and put into a clean pan with the partridge portions. Pour in the sauce and heat gently for 20 to 25 minutes.

Transfer the partridge to a warmed serving dish and pour the sauce around them. Garnish with the watercress and toast.
Serves 2

Guinea Fowl with Raspberries

1 oven-ready guinea
    fowl
salt and pepper
25 g (1 oz) butter
2 rosemary sprigs
175 g (6 oz) fresh or
    frozen raspberries,
    thawed
1 tablespoon oil
4 tablespoons
    raspberry vinegar
4 tablespoons double
    cream
TO GARNISH:
50 g (2 oz) fresh or
    frozen raspberries,
    thawed
parsley sprigs
bay leaves

Season the guinea fowl well inside and out with salt and pepper. Put half the butter, the rosemary and 50 g (2 oz) of the raspberries in the body cavity.

Heat the remaining butter and the oil in a pan, add the guinea fowl and brown on all sides. Add the vinegar.

Lay the guinea fowl on its side and cook for 20 to 25 minutes, then turn onto the other side and cook for a further 20 to 25 minutes. Transfer to a warmed serving dish; keep warm.

Add the cream, and salt and pepper to taste to the pan, stirring well to dissolve the sediment, then add the remaining raspberries and heat through gently, without stirring.

Spoon the raspberry sauce around the guinea fowl. Garnish with the raspberries and herbs. Serve with a mixed salad.
Serves 2 or 4

VENISON, RABBIT & HARE

Venison Steaks in Cream

4 × 175 g (6 oz)
  venison top rump
  steaks
sea salt
8 juniper berries,
  coarsely crushed
2 tablespoons oil
25 g (1 oz) butter
1 tablespoon clear
  honey
2 tablespoons mild
  mustard
4 tablespoons double
  cream
25 g (1 oz) flaked
  almonds, toasted
watercress sprigs to
  garnish

Season the venison steaks with the sea salt and crushed juniper berries, pressing them on firmly. Brush with a little of the oil.

Heat the remaining oil and the butter in a heavy-based frying pan until very hot. Add the steaks and cook for 1 minute on each side, or to taste, pressing down firmly as they cook. Transfer to a warmed serving dish.

Add the honey, mustard and cream to the pan and heat gently, stirring, until smooth. Pour over the steaks, then sprinkle with the almonds.

Garnish with watercress and serve with steamed potatoes tossed in parsley butter, and French beans.
Serves 4

Crumbed Venison Cutlets

8 venison best end
   cutlets
1 clove garlic, halved
4 tablespoons olive
   oil
flour for coating
salt and pepper
2 eggs, beaten
250 g (8 oz) fresh
   white breadcrumbs
4 tablespoons grated
   Parmesan cheese
1 teaspoon ground
   coriander
1 teaspoon paprika
40 g (1½ oz) butter

Rub the venison with the cut garlic. Place the oil in a large flat dish, add the venison and leave for 15 minutes, turning once. Drain well, reserving the oil, and pat dry with kitchen paper. Season the flour with salt and pepper and use to coat the meat, then dip the cutlets in the beaten egg.

Mix the breadcrumbs, Parmesan, coriander and paprika together and use to coat the cutlets, pressing on firmly. Chill for 5 minutes.

Heat the reserved oil and the butter in a roasting pan. Remove from the heat and add the cutlets, turning them over carefully so that both sides are coated in oil. Cook in a preheated hot oven, 220°C (425°F), Gas Mark 7, for 15 to 20 minutes or until golden and crisp.

Serve with hot beetroot tossed in cream, and shredded cabbage.
Serves 4

Butterfly Venison Steaks

4 × 125 g (4 oz)
   venison fillet
   steaks
angostura bitters
salt and white pepper
40 g (1½ oz) butter
1 tablespoon olive oil
2 tablespoons brandy
HORSERADISH
   BUTTER:
25 g (1 oz) butter,
   softened
2 tablespoons
   chopped chives
2 teaspoons grated
   horseradish

First, make the horseradish butter: mix all the ingredients together and shape into a roll. Chill until firm, then slice and cut into shapes.

Cut the venison steaks almost in half horizontally and open out flat to form a 'butterfly' shape; press with the hand to flatten. Sprinkle each with 2 shakes of angostura, and salt and pepper to taste.

Heat the butter and oil in a heavy-based frying pan, add the steaks and fry for 15 seconds on each side, pressing down firmly. Transfer to a warmed serving dish and keep hot.

Remove the pan from the heat and pour in the brandy, stirring to dissolve the sediment. Pour over the steaks and top each with a portion of horseradish butter. Serve with stir-fried mange-tout and game chips*.
Serves 4

NOTE: The meat is perfect cooked so briefly; for more conservative tastes cook the venison for 30 to 45 seconds on each side, no longer.

Venison Loaf

250 g (8 oz) streaky
    bacon, derinded
625 g (1¼ lb) pie
    venison, minced
salt and pepper
1 egg, beaten
250 g (8 oz) fresh
    white breadcrumbs
finely grated or
    shredded rind of
    1 lemon
25 g (1 oz) parsley,
    coarsely chopped
75 g (3 oz) stoned
    black olives

Line the base and sides of a 500 g (1 lb) loaf tin with bacon rashers, stretching them to fit if necessary; chop the remainder and set aside.

Place the venison in a bowl, season with salt and pepper to taste and bind with half the egg. Spread half this mixture over the bacon.

Mix the breadcrumbs, remaining egg, lemon rind, parsley and chopped bacon together and spread half on top of the venison. Press the olives into the mixture. Spread the remaining venison on top and cover with the remaining breadcrumb mixture.

Cover loosely with foil and bake in a preheated moderately hot oven, 190°C (375°F), Gas Mark 5, for 1 hour. Allow to stand for 3 to 4 minutes, then pour off and reserve the juices.

Turn out the terrine onto a serving dish and serve sliced, hot or cold, with the juices. Serve a potato salad, lettuce and a tomato and orange vinaigrette as accompaniments.
Serves 4

Maurice's Hare Pâté

750 g (1½ lb) hare,
    including haunch
    and saddle portion
8 rashers streaky
    bacon, derinded
750 g (1½ lb) fat
    pork, half cubed
    and half minced
2 or 3 bay leaves
MARINADE:
2 tablespoons
    calvados or brandy
150 ml (¼ pint) red
    wine
2 cloves garlic,
    crushed
½ teaspoon coarsely
    grated nutmeg
½ teaspoon ground
    allspice
1½ teaspoons salt
8-10 juniper berries,
    crushed or pounded
6-8 black
    peppercorns,
    crushed or pounded
4-5 thyme sprigs

Using a sharp small-bladed knife, cut the meat from the bones and chop roughly; keep the fillet portions from the saddle whole, slicing them lengthways.

Stretch the bacon with a knife and use to line a 1.5 kg (3 lb) rectangular or oval terrine.

Mix the marinade ingredients together in a large bowl, add the fillet portions and fat pork cubes and leave for 1 hour. Drain and set aside. Add the chopped hare and minced fat pork to the marinade and blend well.

Arrange half the marinated fillet slices in the terrine and cover with half the minced pork and hare mixture; repeat the layers. Cover with the marinated fat pork cubes, pressing down well. Arrange the bay leaves on top.

Cover the terrine securely with foil, or foil and a lid, and place in a roasting pan. Pour enough boiling water into the pan to come halfway up the sides of the terrine. Cook in a preheated moderate oven, 180°C (350°F), Gas Mark 4, for 2 hours. Remove from the pan and leave to stand for 10 to 15 minutes.

Place a flat board and weight on top and leave in the refrigerator for 24 hours.

Turn out the pâté onto a serving dish and serve sliced, with gherkins, pickled onions and toast or hot crisp French bread and butter.
Serves 6

NOTE: If preferred, this pâté can be eaten hot; pour off the juices and serve separately. Serve with broccoli.

Hare Agrodolce

2 tablespoons flour
1/2 teaspoon salt
1 teaspoon dry
  mustard
pepper
4 hare haunch
  portions
25 g (1 oz) butter
1 tablespoon oil
50 g (2 oz) ham
4 button onions
4 cloves
1 clove garlic,
  chopped
bouquet garni
150 ml (1/4 pint) port
4 tablespoons red
  wine vinegar
25 g (1 oz) raisins
25 g (1 oz) plain
  chocolate, grated
parsley to garnish

Season the flour with the salt,
mustard, and pepper to taste and use
to coat the hare.

Heat the butter and oil in a large
pan, add the hare and cook until
browned on both sides.

Cut the ham into thin strips. Stud
each onion with a clove. Add the ham
and onions to the pan with the garlic,
bouquet garni, port, vinegar and
raisins. Bring to simmering point,
cover and cook gently for 50 to
55 minutes or until the meat is very
tender. Remove the hare pieces with a
slotted spoon and arrange on a
warmed serving dish.

Add the chocolate to the sauce,
stirring to dissolve, then pour over
the hare. Garnish with parsley and
serve with buttered noodles and
steamed fennel.
Serves 4

Hare in Ginger Cream Sauce

1 saddle of hare, in
   1 or 2 pieces
2 tablespoons Dijon
   mustard
8 rashers streaky
   bacon, derinded
25 g (1 oz)
   crystallized ginger,
   finely sliced
4 tablespoons
   whipping cream
salt and pepper
MARINADE:
4 juniper berries,
   crushed
1 teaspoon green
   peppercorns,
   crushed
3 tablespoons olive
   oil
3 tablespoons red
   wine
1 onion, sliced

Mix the marinade ingredients in a large non-metal bowl, add the hare and leave for 24 hours. Drain and dry thoroughly; strain the marinade and reserve. Brush the hare with the mustard.

Stretch the bacon rashers with a knife, then wrap around the hare, securing underneath with wooden cocktail sticks. Place in a roasting pan and cook in a preheated moderately hot oven, 200°C (400°F), Gas Mark 6, for 35 to 40 minutes, basting frequently; and a little of the marinade if the pan becomes dry. Transfer the hare to a warmed serving dish; keep hot.

Pour the remaining marinade into the roasting pan and cook on top of the stove, stirring to scrape up the sediment, until thickened. Add the ginger and cream and heat through. Season with salt and pepper to taste.

Serve the hare with potatoes tossed in parsley, and peas. Hand the sauce separately.
Serves 2 to 4

Paprika Rabbit with Herb Dumplings

500 g (1 lb) frozen
  boneless Chinese
  rabbit, thawed
2 teaspoons paprika
2 onions, chopped
2 celery sticks, thinly
  sliced
1 × 539 g
  (1 lb 3 oz) can
  tomatoes
2 teaspoons
  Worcestershire
  sauce
salt and pepper
DUMPLINGS:
50 g (2 oz) self-
  raising flour
pinch of salt
15 g (½ oz) suet or
  butter
2 tablespoons
  chopped chives
2 tablespoons milk

Put the rabbit, paprika, onions, celery, tomatoes with their juice, Worcestershire sauce, and salt and pepper in a large pan. Bring to simmering point, cover and cook gently for 35 minutes.

Meanwhile, make the dumplings. Sift the flour and salt into a bowl and rub in the suet or butter until the mixture resembles breadcrumbs. Stir in the chives, add the milk and mix to a soft dough. Knead lightly and form into 8 to 12 tiny dumplings. Add to the pan, cover and simmer for a further 15 minutes.

Serve the rabbit and dumplings with sliced green beans and cauliflower.
Serves 4

Rabbit and Forcemeat Pie

flour for coating
salt and pepper
1.25 kg (2½ lb)
    rabbit joints
1 tablespoon oil
250 g (8 oz) back
    bacon, derinded
    and chopped
3 hard-boiled eggs,
    quartered
2 leeks, thinly sliced
300 ml (½ pint)
    light stock (approx)
500 g (1 lb) potatoes,
    boiled and sliced
FORCEMEAT BALLS:
250 g (8 oz) pork
    sausage meat
1 tablespoon chopped
    parsley
1 teaspoon chopped
    sage

First, make the forcemeat balls. Place the sausage meat, parsley and sage in a bowl, with salt and pepper to taste. Mix well and form into small balls.

Season the flour with salt and pepper and use to coat the rabbit. Heat the oil in a frying pan, add the bacon and cook until the fat runs; drain and set aside. Add the forcemeat balls to the pan and cook until golden; set aside. Add the rabbit joints, 2 at a time, and cook until lightly coloured.

Arrange half the bacon, rabbit, forcemeat balls, eggs and leeks in a casserole; repeat the layers. Three-quarters fill with stock and top with overlapping potato slices. Cover and cook in a preheated moderate oven, 180°C (350°F), Gas Mark 4, for 20 minutes. Uncover and cook for a further 15 minutes. Serve hot or cold.
Serves 4

Rabbit Casserole

750 g (1½ lb) rabbit
    joints
300 ml (½ pint) red
    wine
rind of 1 lemon
2 cloves garlic, crushed
bouquet garni
250 g (8 oz) cooked
    ham, cubed
250 g (8 oz) onion,
    sliced
250 g (8 oz) carrots,
    thinly sliced
½ teaspoon salt
125 g (4 oz) button
    mushrooms, halved
15 g (½ oz) butter
1 tablespoon flour
¼ teaspoon cayenne
1 tablespoon
    redcurrant jelly

Put the rabbit, wine, lemon rind, garlic, herbs, ham, onion, carrot and salt in a flameproof casserole. Bring to simmering point, cover and cook in a preheated moderate oven, 180°C (350°F), Gas Mark 4, for 35 minutes.

Add the mushrooms and cook for 15 minutes or until the rabbit and vegetables are tender. Using a slotted spoon, transfer meat and vegetables to a warmed serving dish; keep hot.

Soften the butter and mix with the flour to form a paste, then drop small pieces into the liquid in the casserole. Cook, stirring over moderate heat, until thickened and smooth.

Add the cayenne and redcurrant jelly and cook for 3 to 4 minutes, until syrupy. Pour over the meat and vegetables. Serve with dumplings.
Serves 4

INDEX

ACKNOWLEDGMENTS

Photography by Paul Williams
Food prepared by Clare Ferguson
Photographic stylist: Penny Markham
Illustrations by Lindsay Blow